Cumberland

3 1999 00008 805+

W9-BKT-477

amazon
7/14/14
$19.53

ALSO BY ANDREA DI ROBILANT

Irresistible North
Lucia: A Venetian Life in the Age of Napoleon
A Venetian Affair

CHASING THE ROSE

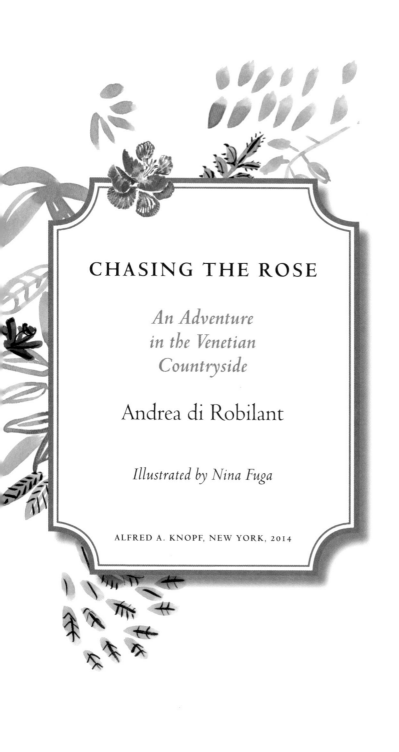

CHASING THE ROSE

*An Adventure
in the Venetian
Countryside*

Andrea di Robilant

Illustrated by Nina Fuga

ALFRED A. KNOPF, NEW YORK, 2014

SB
411.65
O55
D5
2014

THIS IS A BORZOI BOOK
PUBLISHED BY ALFRED A. KNOPF

Copyright © 2014 by Andrea di Robilant

All rights reserved under International and Pan-American Copyright
Conventions. Published in the United States by Alfred A. Knopf,
a division of Random House LLC, New York, and in Canada
by Random House of Canada Limited, Toronto,
Penguin Random House companies.

www.randomhouse.com

Knopf, Borzoi Books, and the colophon are registered trademarks of
Random House LLC.

Library of Congress Cataloging-in-Publication Data
Di Robilant, Andrea, [date]
Chasing the rose : an adventure in the Venetian countryside / by Andrea
di Robilant ; illustrations by Nina Fuga.
pages cm
ISBN 978-0-307-96292-8 (hardcover)—ISBN 978-0-307-96293-5 (eBook)
1. Old Roses—Italy—Venice Region.   2. Roses—Identification.
3. Di Robilant, Andrea, [date].   4. Di Robilant, Andrea [date]—Homes
and haunts—Italy—Venice Region.   5. Gardens—Italy—Venice Region.
6. Memmo Mocenigo, Lucia, 1770–1854—Homes and haunts—Italy—
Venice Region.   7. Josephine, Empress, consort of Napoleon I, Emperor
of the French, 1763–1814.   I. Title.
SB411.65.O55D5 2014
635.9'33734—dc23   2013023994

Jacket art by Nina Fuga
Jacket design by Iris Weinstein

Manufactured in the United Kingdom
First Edition

For my mother, Elizabeth Stokes

CONTENTS

CHASING THE ROSE

CHAPTER ONE

Alvisopoli

It was early summer and the new corn was growing as far as the eye could see on the flat Venetian
mainland. Here and there the distant tip of a bell
tower peeping over the stalks signaled the presence of a

village lying low in that leafy green sea. Driving north from Venice, I kept losing my bearings on the narrow back roads, until a small, rusty sign came into view: ALVISOPOLI 2 KM.

My family's association with this small town had ended nearly a century earlier. Yet the name still had a hold on my imagination, eliciting a strange nostalgia for a world I had never known but with which I felt intensely familiar.

Alvisopoli was the brainchild of my great-great-great-great-grandfather Alvise Mocenigo. At the end of the eighteenth century he reclaimed a vast tract of marshland that belonged to the family and, guided by a pioneering spirit that was truly at odds with the decadent mentality of the old Venetian ruling class, built a model farming and manufacturing community, with proper housing for the workers and their families, health care, and an educational system that included a state-of-the-art technical school. The community grew to become a proper little town, which he named after himself: the "City of Alvise."

After the fall of the Venetian Republic, in 1797, Alvisopoli continued to thrive despite financial difficulties and the ravages of successive wars. In fact, its greatest expansion took place during the time of Napoleon.

But Alvise died prematurely, in 1815, shortly after the collapse of the empire. It fell on his widow, Lucia, and afterward their son, Alvisetto, and his heirs, to carry on his visionary project. As it happened, the utopian ideal and its élan faded during the nineteenth century. Alvisopoli became a farming estate like many others, the only difference being that it was much larger than the other big properties in the region.

My grandfather Andrea di Robilant inherited the property from two childless Mocenigo aunts after World War I. He sold it in the 1930s to pay his debts, and the estate was broken up. The new owners continued to farm the land, but they abandoned the village, including the main villa and the surrounding buildings. For a long time Alvisopoli was little more than a small ghost town, lost in the Venetian countryside. But in the mid-1980s a state agency stepped in to convert the old buildings into a low-income housing project. Some twenty years later, I was driving through that part of the country and decided it was time to make a belated pilgrimage to the old family estate I had heard so much about as a child.

I emerged from the cornfields directly onto the main square of the town and parked the car in front of the old Bar Mocenigo. The layout of the town was intact—no new buildings had been added since the early nineteenth century—but the impression of stepping back in time vanished as soon as I reached the main villa, where the new tenants had moved in. Satellite dishes were secured to the windowsills. Clothes were hanging out to dry. In the back of the main house, the garden had been divided into weedy vegetable plots. There was a melancholy shabbiness about the place that reminded me of Eastern Europe during the Cold War.

I was about to turn away and head to Bar Mocenigo to lift my spirits with a shot of grappa when a short, portly man I took to be the caretaker emerged from the villa amid a loud jangling of keys. "I am Benito Dalla Via," he announced. "Can I be of any help?" His face lit up when I told him my family had lived on the estate for many generations. "Come with me," he said. He took out the batch of keys and led me to the little church that Alvise Mocenigo had commissioned in the early nineteenth century. "Here are the tombs of your ancestors," Benito said as he pointed to the marble slabs under which lay the remains of Alvise and several of his descendants.

It turned out Benito was not the official caretaker, but rather a self-appointed one. The housing board had assigned to him and his wife, Giuditta, a small apartment on the ground floor of the villa. Giuditta pruned and watered the plants in the condominium courtyard.

Benito, a retired hotel porter with time on his hands, had taken up embroidery. The walls in the sitting room where I was invited for coffee were covered with framed renderings of flowerpots, biblical scenes, and Venetian vistas.

After coffee, Benito rose to his feet and commanded me to follow him. "I am taking you to the park," he said, and led me past the vegetable plots behind the villa to a peeling old gate. He pulled out another set of keys, and we entered a very thick wood with tall trees, brambles, rotting lumber, and stagnant waters. There were occasional signs of a grander past: a gnarled box-wood hedge, a broken bench, and here and there the traces of an old pathway. But the park had long reverted to wilderness.

As we made our way into the scrub, I realized Benito was looking for something specific he wanted to show me. Soon he came to a halt in a clearing and pointed in the direction of a bush about three feet high that was covered with the loveliest pink roses. As the sur-roundings came into focus, I spotted similar rose shrubs growing in the vicinity, as if a secret garden had sprung up in those woods over the years.

I walked over to the closest plant and took a rose in my hand. It was silvery pink, very light at the center and darker on the outside. The diameter was about three inches. The petals were loose, and fell to the ground as I observed the flower. The scent was very strong and reminded me of peaches and raspberries. Although I did not know much about roses, everything about this one—the delicate color, the sweet fragrance, the way it carried itself—suggested this was an old rose of some importance that had been growing wild in these woods for a very long time. Its presence was mysterious yet assertive.

"We call it 'Rosa Moceniga,' but so far no one has been able to identify it or to explain why it grows here at Alvisopoli," Benito said, hoping I might have some inkling.

Giuditta, a shy, soft-spoken woman, had made several cuttings of the rose, which she grew in pots outside their apartment, in the courtyard of the villa. As I prepared to leave, Benito handed me a small plant wrapped in a white plastic bag. "Take it with you," he said. "It will remind you of this place." I promised I would put it in the ground as soon as I got home.

I have a small garden in Venice, on the island of the Giudecca. I am ashamed to say I had left it to itself in the damp climate of the lagoon, so it was in very poor shape at the time. The lawn was beaten up and mossy;

the boxwood hedge around it was overgrown, and the hydrangeas sagged mournfully in the shade. Pots with stunted camellias and dried-up geraniums were scattered about. Every summer, the vine over the pergola went on a rampage, climbing over the wall and into my neighbor's apple trees. It was such a shabby place that I had come to think of it more as an "outdoors" than as a proper garden—a place to store brooms and the occasional garbage bag when I missed the early morning pickup barges.

When I got back home from my visit to Alvisopoli, I dug a hole in a sunny spot and stuck the little rose plant in the ground, hoping for the best. I never fed it fertilizer, never pruned it, never even bothered to pull out the weeds that grew around it. Yet it did very well, turning into a graceful little shrub that flowered generously all through the autumn. In the winter, when most of its foliage was gone and the *bora,* the freezing wind from the north, swept across the lagoon,

the plant clung to the hardened ground with the tenacity of a true survivor. I watched it from the window as it battled on, wondering how it could possibly make it through the winter. But the cold went away, and soon the hardy shrub stretched out its bat-tered limbs. And in a matter of days it was covered with buds that were bursting to bloom.

In the spring, I cleaned the place up, kept the hedge fairly well groomed, and filled my pots with clematis and scented geraniums. I even took out the moss and reseeded the lawn. As the mysterious rose continued to thrive, its sweet fragrance mixing with the salty air of the lagoon, I thought the least I could do was provide it with decent surroundings.

Malmaison

For a while I didn't give much thought to the Rosa Moceniga. The shrub continued to grow, and to flower generously from early March to late November, and I was quite happy to leave

 it at that, enjoying the slight air of mystery that hung over those fragrant pink blossoms. Then a chance discovery in the Venice Archives suddenly opened up a trail that proved irresistible.

I was going through some old family manuscripts one day when a large notebook, tattered and worn around the edges, slipped out of a folder and fell to the ground. It turned out to be a diary of my great-great-great-great-grandmother Lucia Mocenigo, which she kept while living in Paris in the waning days of Napoleon's empire. I sat down to read the entries she had written so diligently in her tiny scrawl. To my surprise, I was transported to a world that seemed in the throes of a mad love affair with roses even as it was falling apart.

Lucia moved to Paris in the summer of 1813 to be with her son, Alvisetto, who was enrolled in a Parisian lycée. Her husband, Alvise, the founder of Alvisopoli, was a senator in the Kingdom of Italy, the puppet state Napoleon had created in northern Italy after the fall of the Venetian Republic. The emperor expected prominent figures in his various European dominions to send their male children to school in France, so as to forge them into loyal subjects of the empire. Lucia had resisted sending her son away, relenting only on the condition that she be able to join him.

She did not have many friends in Paris, but one of them was Empress Josephine, who had set up court at the Château de Malmaison after Napoleon divorced her on the grounds that she could not give him an heir. Lucia had met Josephine briefly in Venice, at the time of Napoleon's conquest of the Venetian Republic in 1797. They renewed their friendship in Milan, in the early years of the empire, when Lucia was lady-in-waiting at the court of Viceroy Eugène de Beauharnais, Josephine's son. In 1810, after the imperial divorce, Lucia and Alvise attended the wedding of Napoleon and Marie Louise, the eighteen-year-old archduchess of Austria, as part of the official Italian delegation. At the risk of being frowned upon at court, Lucia took the opportunity of visiting Josephine in the small, run-down Château de Navarre, where the emperor had exiled his former wife for the duration of the wedding festivities. And Josephine appreciated the gesture.

When Lucia arrived in Paris in 1813, she had not seen Josephine in nearly three years. Shortly after settling into a small apartment in Faubourg Saint-Germain, she

took her carriage out to Malmaison to visit the former empress. She gives a funny description of their encounter. Josephine was waiting for them in the new billiard room, near the entrance hall with its stark white-and-black checkered floor, green wallpaper, and Egyptian decorations. A small parrot with colorful plumage was perched on Josephine's breast. As Lucia and Alvisetto walked in, the parrot started furiously pecking the flowers of a small bouquet fixed in Josephine's hair. The empress did not lose her calm, but the greetings had to be interrupted while she removed three strings of pearls from around her neck for fear that the parrot should take aim at them, too. It was time enough for Lucia, always a keen observer, to take a close look at the splendid pearls and value them at "no less than one hundred thousand francs."

Malmaison became a second home to Lucia. The atmosphere was easy and relaxing. There were usually no more than a few close friends and members of the family in attendance. On weekends, Lucia occasionally took Alvisetto to play with Josephine's grandchildren (the son and daughter of Hortense, queen of Holland). The adults played Boston (Josephine's favorite card game) and, when the weather was nice, took walks around the estate.

The garden had been landscaped *à l'anglaise* by the Scottish horticulturist and garden designer Thomas Blaikie, a favorite of Marie Antoinette's before the Revolution, and Lucia loved the way it blended naturally with the surrounding farmland.

Josephine's interest in plants was wide-ranging, and the grounds and greenhouses at Malmaison were filled with exotic species of all kinds, including her collections of heathers, succulent plants, and *Pelargonia*. But she was obsessed with roses. She started out modestly enough, with twenty-six fairly common species, which she placed in clusters around the estate to create a natural effect. But soon the collector's spirit took over, and she began to accumulate increasingly rare cultivars, which she kept in pots lined up in her greenhouses. By the time Lucia visited Malmaison, Josephine's collection included more than two hundred different species and varieties, and was the envy of the *grandes dames* of the empire.

Josephine had unlimited means at her disposal to indulge her passion, and she went out of her way to obtain rare roses she did not yet have. Her main provider was André Du Pont, possibly the greatest collector of his time. An employee with the postal service, he was also the *serviteur des roses* at the Jardin des Plantes, the prime institution for the study of natural sciences. But Josephine also ordered roses from abroad. Lee and Kennedy, a famous nursery in Hammersmith, was a regular supplier.

Josephine was especially eager to get her hands on the fabulous roses coming from China to England often via Calcutta, where the plants rested in a large garden set up by the British East India Company. The British had a monopoly on the Chinese plant importation, the French having been cut out ever since the Compagnie des Indes, the equivalent of the flourishing East India Company, went bankrupt during the Revolution. But that did not stop Josephine from getting what she wanted. Not even war diminished her appetite. When she heard that the coveted *R. indica odorata* (later to be known as 'Hume's Blush Tea-Scented China') was on its way from the Fa Tee Nursery in Canton to Sir Abraham Hume's garden in Hertfordshire, she made sure arrangements between the French and British admiralties were set up so that a specimen was sent to her.

After Napoleon imposed the Continental Blockade on Great Britain, Josephine convinced the emperor to give John Kennedy, the Hammersmith nurseryman, a special permit so that he could cross the Channel and come to Malmaison with his seeds and plants. The year Lucia settled in Paris, Kennedy provided Josephine with at least four new Chinese roses that had recently arrived in England via the East India Company. These were *R. chinensis*, *R. multiflora*, and *R. chinensis semperflorens*— this last being the Chinese horticultural variety that brought the color red to European roses and was named Slater's Crimson China after one of the directors of the East India Company, Gilbert Slater.

Lucia was not by inclination a collector, and as far as I know, her love of roses never became an obsession as it did for so many of her contemporaries. But in Josephine's company she developed an interest in botany that she had never really shown before her trip to Paris. Josephine encouraged her to pursue it seriously, introducing her to René Desfontaines, the longtime chair of botanical studies at the Jardin des Plantes.

Professor Desfontaines gave Lucia a personal tour of the Jardin des Plantes on their first meeting. He showed her, among other things, an extensive collection of exotic wood, an herb garden with twenty thousand specimens, underground mushroom galleries, and a section devoted to the fruits of rare plants, including that of the breadfruit tree, which, Lucia noted with amazement, "can be sliced as a loaf and cooked in the oven."

The eminent botanist took Lucia under his wing. She joined his class, which met every day in a large theater at the Jardin des Plantes. "We were twelve ladies in all, seated in the lower part of the theater," she reported after her first lesson. "The men, mostly young, stood behind a low balustrade." There were a couple of foreign military officers and, she recognized right behind her, the composer Luigi Cherubini, who was out of favor as a musician and had decided to wait it out, as it were, by starting his own herb garden. "As soon as the lesson was over," Lucia went on, "the ladies leapt from their chairs and led the assault on the plants and flowers that had been made available for the students. By the time I managed to get to the front, none were left. I was new and didn't know better, but I'll certainly make sure I get my share of pots in the future."

Lucia studied hard and rarely missed a class. She understood how privileged she was to be studying botany with Desfontaines. The atmosphere at the Jardin des Plantes inspired her, and she spent more and more time there. André Thouin, the legendary chief gardener, gave her private lessons on everything from planting techniques to the preparation of fertilizers. At Josephine's urging, Lucia went to see her rose provider, Monsieur Du Pont, who taught her the art of grafting. She also paid regular visits to the nursery on rue Saint-Jacques that belonged to Louis Noisette—Louis and his brother

Philippe later gave their name to an entire family of roses.

Josephine's passion for roses sparked considerable competition among the ladies of the empire, who liked to show off their gardens and point out their rare cultivars. It was said that Parisian society was gripped by "*rosomanie,*" a term coined to describe that obsessive new love. Lucia gladly accepted invitations for lunch or for afternoon lemonade if there was a good chance that an instructive walk in the garden would follow. She particularly enjoyed visiting Madame Crawford, an old friend of Josephine's who lived on rue d'Anjou, in the district around Faubourg-Saint-Honoré. Madame Crawford was in her sixties but still beautiful and very much the *grande dame,* despite her adventurous, scandal-ridden past. In fact, the story of her fascinating life was as much a draw for Lucia as her beautiful roses.

Born Anna Eleonora Franchi in a small town in Tuscany, she was already acting and dancing on the stage at fifteen. The Duke of Württemberg noticed her during the Carnival in Venice and took her back to Vienna. She bore him two illegitimate children before he dumped her. Agile dancer that she was, she landed on her feet, ensnaring Emperor Joseph II, no less. Old Maria Theresa, the dowager empress, banished her from the Austrian Empire. Undaunted, she arrived in Paris on the arm of a new lover, one Maret d'Aigremont, whom she soon dropped in favor of an Englishman by the name of Sullivan; they married and left for Asia with the British East India Company. There Mrs. Sullivan finally met her match: Quentin Crawford, a Scottish banker and businessman known as the Manila Nabob. They returned to Europe and settled in Paris. Crawford continued to enrich himself, and became Marie Antoinette's financial adviser. When the Revolution broke out, the Crawfords remained firmly in the royalist camp, helping Louis XVI and Marie Antoinette make their fateful escape to Varennes. (It was Anna Eleonora who hired the carriage and fetched the false passports for the king and the queen at the Russian embassy.) The Crawfords fled to Brussels to escape the guillotine, returning to Paris in 1795 after Talleyrand pulled a few strings on their behalf. Still flush with money, they installed themselves in the huge Hôtel de Matignon. Talleyrand bought it from them in 1808, and they moved into his former *petit hôtel* on rue d'Anjou, where Madame Crawford began to cultivate her famous rose garden.

"Today it was just the two of us," Lucia wrote in her diary after one of her visits, delighting in the intimacy she had developed with this remarkable woman. On

that particular day, at the end of their customary walk in
the garden, Madame Crawford showed Lucia an R. *multiflora carnea,* which had been recently introduced in
Europe from China and was still quite rare among roses
grown in Paris. It was a sweet-scented flower, fully dou-
ble and globular; the petals were creamy white with a
hint of pink. Madame Crawford instructed her gardener
to prepare a cutting for Lucia to take back to Italy.

Later, Lucia took the cutting and a few sample flowers over to Louis Noisette, on rue Saint-Jacques. The
nurseryman took a close look and shrugged, boasting
that he'd had a similar rose in his nursery "for at least
three years." He told Lucia that his brother Philippe
Noisette, who had a well-known nursery in Charleston,
South Carolina, had obtained seeds directly from China
and had sent one hundred and fifty plants to England,
several of which had found their way to the nursery on
rue Saint-Jacques, in defiance of the blockade. If Noisette's story about the R. *multiflora carnea* was true, we
can safely say he chose not to share the rose with Josephine, who received it from Kennedy only in 1813.

At the height of *rosomanie,* establishing who introduced what rose and when seemed all-important. So it
is worth noting in passing that in his effort to impress
Lucia, the great Noisette neglected to mention that he

had not, in fact, introduced the *R. multiflora carnea* in France. That merit belonged to Jean-François Boursault, a former actor (stage name Malherbe, or "the Weed") who made his fortune during the Revolution with lucrative contracts from the municipal government. Having purchased a large property in the rue Blanche, in the Quartier Pigalle, he built immense greenhouses and filled them with plants from all over the world. His gardens were open to the public and attracted throngs of visitors. Although Boursault knew very little of botany or horticulture, he had a genuine passion for plants and a natural breeder's instinct. He was also a clever schemer, with deep pockets, and managed to smuggle the rare *R. multiflora carnea* from England as early as 1808, a good five years before Josephine received it from Kennedy. Boursault never revealed how he was able to circumvent the blockade, but the contraband of roses across the Channel was clearly flourishing in those years.

*I*n the spring of 1814, Napoleon's empire collapsed. Alexander I occupied Paris at the head of the allied forces. During his stay, the "Emperor of All Russias" paid several courtesy visits to Josephine at Malmaison. One evening, she caught a chill while walking in the garden in his company, never recovered, and died shortly of pneumonia, to the consternation of Lucia and the former empress's many loyal friends.

Once the Bourbon monarchy was restored, there was no reason for Lucia to keep Alvisetto in a French lycée. It was time to go home and join her husband in Alvisopoli. Eager to put to good use all she had learned, she made plans to plant roses around the villa; she also had in mind to transform the woods behind the house into a romantic park.

The time came for her farewell rounds at the Jardin des Plantes. As a graduation gift, Desfontaines gave her a copy of Auguste Plée's *Le jeune botaniste*, a popular book among aspiring gardeners. Plée, a French botanist who lived in Guadeloupe, wrote the book in the form of a correspondence between father and son, and Desfontaines thought it might come in handy for Alvisetto, whom Lucia had often brought to the lectures.

After handing Lucia her diploma, Desfontaines drew up a list of trees, shrubs, and flowers that he thought would do well in Alvisopoli. André Thouin, the chief gardener, gave her a pass to the seed house, where she had permission to take all she needed. She also paid one more visit to Monsieur Du Pont, for some last-minute advice on the cultivation of roses. Meanwhile, at the nursery on rue Saint-Jacques, Monsieur Noisette filled crates and boxes with the plants on the list prepared by Desfontaines. The list, alas, is lost, so I have only a very limited idea of the roses Lucia might have brought back to Italy. In addition to the *R. multiflora carnea*, which Noisette expressly grafted for her, she mentions in her diary a "rose panachée" (perhaps an *R. gallica versicolor*, also known at the time as a *rosier à fleur panachée*), a "rose anemone" (perhaps the great hybridizer Jacques-Louis Descemet's "rose à forme d'anémone," a Gallica rose), and a "rose à carafe" (perhaps another of Descemet's Gallicas, listed in his catalog as "ornement de carafe"). Lucia mentions two roses that came from Du Pont's collection: 'La Belle Laure', an *R. pimpinellifolia*, now extinct, and 'Mère Gigogne', a Gallica first obtained by Descemet.

Lucia left Paris at the end of August 1814, taking with her a botanical collection that included rose seeds, rose cuttings, and small rose plants. Her diary ends with her voyage home. As I returned the manuscript to the stacks at the archives, this much was now clear: the Rosa Moceniga growing wild at Alvisopoli was one of the roses Lucia had brought back from Paris in one of the wobbling crates piled high in the luggage carriage.

*T*he estate to which Lucia returned was in terrible shape. First the French troops and then the invading Austrians had trampled the fields, destroyed crops, cut down trees for firewood, and emptied all the grain stores. Her husband, Alvise, was very ill, and died within a year, leaving her the burden of saving the property. For the sake of Alvisetto, she took on the challenge. After a few very tough years, Alvisopoli gradually came back to life. Only then did Lucia turn to the task of embellishing the grounds with the plants she had brought from France.

She cleared the existing woods behind the villa of brambles and brush but left the big native trees, including planes, hornbeams, oaks, ilexes, elms, ashes, and beeches. She added some North American varieties brought back from Paris: silver and red maples, canoe birches, Eastern red cedars, and American sweet gums. Next came pathways and canals with running water that poured into a large pond in the center of the park. Every path was lined with tall boxwood hedges; marble statues were placed along the pathway; and bridges were built over the canals. The excess earth from the canals was used to erect three hillocks in different parts of the park, topped, respectively, by an ilex, an oak, and a plane tree. A spiral path around each mound led to a belvedere. In the center of the park was a large pond with an islet that could be reached in a rowboat. Rose-bushes and shrubs were scattered around the grounds in clusters for color and decoration. No doubt Professor Desfontaines and the rest of Lucia's friends at the Jardin des Plantes would have been proud of her accomplishment.

The park thrived for two more generations, even surviving the ravages of World War I, when the Italian army requisitioned the property to garrison troops fighting the Austrians. But my grandfather, who inherited the property immediately after the war, had little patience with farming. He lived the high life in the 1920s, and by the time the 1930s came around, he was so ridden with debt that he was forced to sell Alvisopoli. Lucia's lovely park was left untended and soon reverted to wilderness. For a long time the only visitors were the children of the nearby village, who climbed trees and splashed in the stagnant, slimy waters of the old pond during the hot summers.

It was not until the early 1980s that a young forestry student from the university in Padua, Ivo Simonella, wandered into those woods, drawn by the intriguing diversity of the vegetation. He returned again and again, making his way into the thicket and across the big pond and up the hills and over canals and fallen trees. He became obsessed with the place and decided to write his thesis on the trees of Alvisopoli. Every day, he would drive out with his measuring cord to map the area and make a careful census. Simonella's father, who had recently retired, often came along for the exercise and the fresh air; he'd stand in the brambles holding the cord while his son took measurements and jotted down his comments.

"In the end I registered one thousand and ninety-seven trees," Simonella told me when I caught up with him many years later, in Portogruaro, a river town fifteen minutes east of Alvisopoli, where he worked as the local commissioner for the environment. "I remember every single one."

We sat in a café under a large elm tree in the town's lovely public park. Simonella was a lanky, taciturn fellow with thick glasses and an unruly beard. By way of introduction, he told me he preferred the company of trees to that of human beings. On Facebook, where I had first made contact with him, he used to go by the name of Ivo the Bear.

Simonella recalled that the state housing agency had begun to convert the villa into low-income apartments just as he was finishing up his tree count in the woods.

"I convinced the new management that spending a little money to clear the brush and unclog the canals was worthwhile," he said. The local chapter of the World Wildlife Fund then agreed to manage the park as a public space, and Simonella was put in charge. He enlisted young conscientious objectors—military service was still compulsory in Italy in the 1980s, and many people avoided conscription by doing social work—to dig new canals, clear brush, and restore pathways and bridges.

One day, after the new tenants had moved into the renovated apartments, Simonella found Benito Dalla Via wandering in the park. "He'd come to watch us work and would follow us around," he told me. "He asked a lot of questions and seemed to have a genuine interest in the plants that grew at Alvisopoli. In fact, he became quite knowledgeable about the local habitat."

Funds soon dried up, and the WWF was forced to withdraw from the project. Simonella dismissed the volunteers and quit his job. "It was all very sudden. One day I simply locked the gate to the woods and moved on. I left the keys with Benito. I figured that, having spent a lifetime as a hotel porter, he'd know what to do with them."

CHAPTER THREE

The Rose Planter

Back in the days when he was digging ditches and clearing scrub at Alvisopoli, Simonella sometimes bumped into Paolo De Rocco, a local architect and landscaper lured to the same woods by the pink rose shrubs. In fact, it was De Rocco who drew the attention of Simonella, a tree man at heart, to those mysterious roses that grew under his very nose.

De Rocco recognized the plant right away (by observing the shape of the flower and the bearing of the plant) as a Chinese rose of some significance. He returned to Alvisopoli hoping to identify it and to understand why it was there. He called it Rosa Moceniga, by simple association with the refurbished eighteenth-century villa he could glimpse through the trees. "It was meant as a study name, to be used until I figured out what it was," he told me years later.

I met De Rocco twice, both times in connection with Alvisopoli. He was in his early sixties, not very tall, and slightly stooped, as if he carried a huge weight on his shoulders. He smoked and talked—always about plants and how nobody seemed to care much for them. Occasionally I would get a call from him and he would complain about the deteriorating conditions of the park. The last time he phoned, he was very upset because the state agency that managed the property had contracted a lumber company to come in with bulldozers and tear down all the trees. To his credit, he raised such hell with the local press that the agency backed out before major damage was done.

De Rocco died of a heart attack shortly after that episode. I knew him only slightly, but later I often found myself following in his footsteps. He did not have a garden of his own. (When he died, although still married to his wife, Costanza, he was living alone in a small apartment in the town of San Vito al Tagliamento, ten miles north of Alvisopoli.) So he took to planting roses in other people's gardens, or in town squares, along public roads, and, most often, in country graveyards. His day job was in the field of restoration: crumbling villas, old churches, government houses in need of a facelift. Once the work was finished he would pick out an old rose he thought was especially appropriate for the place and plant a few shrubs or climbers along the walls or in small patches next to the buildings. Nobody asked him to do it, but nobody complained, either.

My favorite De Rocco story is about an old rose he planted on the grave of Pier Paolo Pasolini, the writer and movie director. Pasolini grew up in the small town of Casarsa della Delizia, up the road from San Vito. As a young man in the early 1950s, he was forced to leave town on a wave of homophobia. He moved to Rome with his mother, Susanna, a woman of character who stood by her son. There he threw himself into the vibrant postwar literary scene. By the mid-1960s he was a celebrated author and an outspoken, influential public figure. His remarkable life was cut short in 1975, when he was brutally murdered by a young male prostitute in Ostia, on the Roman seaside. (The circumstances remain murky to this day.) His body was brought back

to Casarsa, where attitudes had changed since the big-
oted 1950s—a large crowd turned up at the burial.

When Pasolini was growing up, his mother kept a
vegetable garden where she also planted flowers. Her
favorite was a purple rose known among their neighbors as *la Rosa di Susanna*. (The women traded old
country roses, and the name of the original owner
usually stuck.) When she moved to Rome with her
son, the rose was left to fend for itself among the
weeds and brambles of the old patch. Years later, long
after Pasolini's death, the family home was turned
into a museum. De Rocco, remembering the story of
Susanna's rose, went over to check out the old garden,
which was half-buried under debris from the construction work on the house. Happily, a few purple roses had
survived. He made some cuttings and later planted the
rose on the grave where Pasolini lies buried next to his
mother. The rose flowers every year. As far as I know,
nobody has yet identified it, and the townsfolk still call
it *la Rosa di Susanna*.

Chinese roses—such as the Rosa Moceniga found
by De Rocco at Alvisopoli—were hardly known

in Europe until the second half of the eighteenth century, when trade opened up with Asia, and Europeans discovered the great nurseries of Canton. China was always blessed with roses. Of the two hundred known species in the world, half are native to that country. By the time the Europeans traders arrived, the Chinese had been cultivating and breeding roses for more than two thousand years.

Of course it is possible, even probable, that a few Chinese roses arrived in Europe before the eighteenth century, thanks to monks who traveled to the East. Charles Chamberlain Hurst, an influential geneticist and rose breeder of the first half of the twentieth century, was convinced that a reflowering pink China was cultivated in Renaissance Italy. Hurst based his claim on a mid-sixteenth-century mannerist painting by Bronzino, now at the National Gallery in London, *Venus, Cupid, Folly, and Time*, which shows a smiling putto clutching a fistful of petals he is about to throw at Venus while Cupid kisses her on the mouth. "The small rose pink flowers with translucent petals, incurved stamens, reflexed sepals and small firm ovate shining leaflet," Hurst wrote, "are precisely those of the Pink China." But a painting, even a masterpiece, can hardly be used as scientific evidence. I was more intrigued by a brief entry in the diary that Michel de Montaigne, the great French essayist, kept during his travels in Italy in 1581. In Ferrara, he was taken to a Jesuate monastery—the Jesuates, whose order was founded in 1360 and abolished in 1668, are often confused with the better-known Jesuits—where the monks proudly showed off a reflowering rose. "The shrub produces flowers every month of the year," Montaigne marveled. "I was given a rose that happened to be in bloom." Alas, he did not say what color it was or describe the scent, but it probably *was* a Chinese rose, for no other rose in Italy at the time flowered every month of the year.

These early arrivals, however, were sporadic; they did not influence the development of roses. It was only in the second half of the eighteenth century, when European botanists, nurserymen, and rose breeders "discovered" the China rose, that its potential was fully grasped. Linnaeus, the great Swedish botanist, was probably the first European to catalog a reflowering pink China—*R. indica*, later named 'Hume's Blush Tea-Scented China'—after one of his students, Pehr Osbeck, traveled to Canton and brought a specimen back to Uppsala in 1752. In the following decades, the arrival of different horticultural varieties from China set off a breeding frenzy that led to the introduction of new colors and new scents, not to mention remontancy—a plant's ability to reflower during much of the year. This revolution led to the development of teas and hybrid perpetuals, and eventually to the modern hybrid teas.

The interest of rose historians and breeders has focused on four Chinese roses: the so-called stud Chinas, which arrived in Europe during a thirty-year period and radically transformed the old world of European roses.

In 1792, Gilbert Slater, a nurseryman from Knotts Green, Leyton, introduced a dark, rich crimson rose known in China as Yue Yue Hong, or "Monthly Crimson." Europeans had never seen a rose of that color (called pigeon's blood). The cultivar, which became known as 'Slater's Crimson China', quickly spread to France and then to the rest of the Continent. It became the ancestor of many of the red roses we have today.

Around the time that 'Slater's Crimson China' arrived in Europe, Sir George Staunton, a young diplomat and enthusiastic gardener, traveled to China as secretary to Lord Macartney. Taking time off from his embassy, he went looking for roses and found a lovely reflowering, silvery pink specimen in a Canton nursery, which he shipped to Sir Joseph Banks, the powerful director of the Royal Botanic Gardens at Kew. A year later, in 1793, a Mr. Parsons, who presumably received the seeds or a cutting from Banks, grew the rose in his garden at Rickmansworth, in Hertfordshire. Initially named 'Parsons's Pink China', it later took on the name 'Old Blush'. This rose was the same as, or very similar to, the one brought back by Osbeck.

In 1809, Sir Abraham Hume, a wealthy English rose collector, imported from China a light pink tea-scented specimen (*R. indica odorata*). It so enthused Empress Josephine that she made sure a cultivar was diverted to Malmaison, despite the Continental Blockade imposed by Napoleon. 'Hume's Blush Tea-Scented China' and other new arrivals were crossed with European roses and produced a new family, the teas.

The fourth "stud China" was a very light yellow and smelled of water rose. John Damper Parks brought it back in 1824 for the Royal Horticultural Society. 'Parks' Yellow Tea-Scented China' (*R. indica sulphurea*), which is now considered extinct, is the parent, or ancestor, of many yellow teas and hybrid teas.

All four studs were old Chinese horticultural varieties—probably crosses between the China rose (*R. chinensis*) and the *R. gigantea*, the tea rose of southwest China known as the giant rose because of its large petals and natural tendency to climb as high as forty feet.

Of the four studs, 'Old Blush' is by far the most common today. One finds it in gardens all over the world, its lovely pink flowers providing smudges of color even during the gray winter months. The shrub does well in most climates, roots easily, and requires very little pruning—qualities that help explain its lasting success. The Chinese call it Yue Yue Fen, or "Monthly Pink." There is a painting in the Chinese collection in the Metropolitan Museum of Art depicting a long horizontal branch laden with luscious 'Old Blush' flowers set against a gold background; a wasp nest hangs from one of the lower stems while a dozen wasps hover about, drowsy with nectar. The painting was originally attributed to Zhao Chang, an artist who was active around the tenth to eleventh century. This led some rose historians to say that 'Old Blush' was at least a thousand years old. But the Met experts now believe the painting dates from the Qing Dynasty, which ruled from the seventeenth century. So no one is sure how old this rose is, but it was widely known in China long before George Staunton shipped it to Kew in 1792.

After Mr. Parsons successfully introduced it in his garden at Rickmansworth, 'Old Blush' quickly spread beyond Hertfordshire. James Colville, a nurseryman on the Kings Road in London, sold large quantities of it to France and also to America, where John Champneys, a rice merchant from Charleston, South Carolina, crossed it with 'Old White Musk', a rose from the Himalayas, obtaining 'Champneys' Pink Cluster'. Champneys then gave a seedling to his neighbor Philippe Noisette, a French horticulturist who had emigrated to the United States after the French Revolution, and who, in turn, sent seeds to his brother Louis, the nurseryman from whom Lucia bought her roses in Paris. As a result, 'Champneys' Pink Cluster' is often referred to as the first of a series classified as Noisette roses, and is known as America's main contribution to the evolution of rose breeding.

The story goes that by 1810, 'Old Blush' had reached the island of Bourbon (Réunion) in the Indian Ocean, where French colonists used it to make rose hedges. There it crossed naturally with 'Autumn Damask', eventually generating another important family, the Bourbon roses. In fact, this old China stud has had such a pervasive impact around the world that there are traces of it in the gene pool of most modern roses.

'Old Blush' also happens to be very prolific on the Venetian mainland. When De Rocco first saw the pink rose shrubs at Alvisopoli, he assumed they were 'Old Blush' strays that had found a congenial habitat. Superficially, the two roses look very much alike. The silvery pink flowers are similar, as are the shape and habit of the shrub. The leaves are the same green, and the stems bear thorns that are reddish and fairly sparse. But as De Rocco observed the rose more closely on his return visits, he noticed significant differences, and began to wonder whether these were mere variations due to the conditions of that particular environment or whether he was in the presence of some other, unidentified rose. The Rosa Moceniga had fewer petals, and the flowers were not as round or cuplike as those of the 'Old Blush'. The leaves were not as smooth and shiny. And then, of course, there was the matter of the fragrance: 'Old Blush' had a bland scent that vaguely brought to mind the smell of sweet peas, while the Rosa Moceniga had a very powerful, fruity bouquet.

De Rocco consulted the best nurseries in the region; he called on botanists at universities and research centers; he pestered all the rose growers he knew. But the answer was always the same: it was an 'Old Blush'— with some minor differences perhaps, but an 'Old Blush' all the same.

Not satisfied, De Rocco decided to plant a Rosa Moceniga next to an 'Old Blush', to see if the differences persisted in the same environment. He had the perfect place in mind: a few years earlier he had landscaped the grounds around the ruins of a medieval castle near the hamlet of Fratta, not far from Alvisopoli; along the perimeter of the ruins, he had planted an entire row of 'Old Blush'. One evening after work, he drove up to Fratta with a Rosa Moceniga in the back of his car. He parked in the fields and left the vehicle's floodlights on while he dug a hole at the end of the row of 'Old Blush' and planted the rose he had brought up from Alvisopoli.

When I heard about De Rocco's nighttime mission—this was sometime after he had passed away—I decided to go check on the results of his experiment. The ruins of Fratta are a historical landmark: on those grounds, Ippolito Nievo, a nineteenth-century novelist, set his *Le confessioni di un italiano* (Confessions of an Italian), one of the seminal books of the Italian Risorgimento. Now I had an added reason to make my first patriotic visit to Fratta.

It turned out there were very few ruins left, and none aboveground. But the dozens of different rose shrubs De Rocco had planted years before were now fully grown, and they formed a lovely garden that floated like a dream in the open countryside. I found the row of 'Old Blush' easily enough—the big, sturdy shrubs, covered with pink festoons, always stand out in the distance. And sure enough, at the very end of the hedge was a fully grown Rosa Moceniga—clearly the odd one in the group, even to my untrained eye.

On the way back to Venice, I resolved to have the two roses tested in a lab and to get the matter straightened out once and for all. I called Stefano Mancuso, a professor of botany at the University of Florence, whom I had met in the days when I worked as a reporter for the daily *La Stampa*. Back then he had been doing some pioneering work in the field of plant neurobiology; I'd interviewed him a couple of times, and we had remained on friendly terms. Now I asked him if he had a simple way of determining whether two roses were, in fact, different.

He told me a DNA test would not be conclusive and suggested an alternative testing method he had applied successfully to identify olive trees. The method, he said, was based on a model known as an artificial neural network (ANN)—the same technology that is used in advanced security systems to "recognize" human beings.

"ANN uses software designed to emulate the way a human brain recognizes a person," Mancuso explained. "If a friend of ours grows a beard and puts on twenty pounds, he will look different, but we will recognize him nonetheless. This is because our brain looks at the relationship between the various morphological traits rather than the traits themselves." Mancuso had developed a model that used the same principle to identify plants. It had the additional advantage of resolving the problem of slight morphological variations caused by the environment. For example, two 'Old Blushes' might look a little different depending on the quality of the soil, of the air, of the light. ANN would disregard those differences the same way it would disregard a suntan or a mustache on a human.

"All the information we need is in the leaves," he said. "I'll need sixty for each plant. Make sure you bring me two cuttings that I can use."

It was January, and most rosebushes were bare. Fortunately, the shrub in my garden in Venice had not lost all its leaves. There were little cherry-pink buds as well, and orange hips that dangled like earrings. I clipped off a generous cutting, wrapped one end with wet cotton, and headed to Florence. It was a three-hour drive on the autostrada, across the snow-covered Apennines. Occasionally I checked the backseat to make sure my sample was not wilting.

Mancuso's lab was at the university's research center in Sesto Fiorentino, a northern suburb of Florence. I took an early exit and made a detour to Barni, a well-known rose nursery near Pistoia, where I purchased the last 'Old Blush' of the season. With two roses now in the backseat, I headed to my appointment.

When I arrived, Mancuso, a tweedy Tuscan in his early forties sporting a neatly trimmed beard, was in his lab hovering over a tray of baby *Paulownia*. "We've been tracking their communication patterns," he said, extending his hand to me. I had recently watched him on YouTube deliver a TED lecture on the language of plants.

"Why *Paulownia*s?" I asked.

"They are chatterboxes," he said. "They never shut up."

I handed over the samples, and Mancuso explained the procedure. First he was going to determine eighteen morphological parameters, such as area, perimeter, major and minor axis length, roundness, elongation, and compactness. Half the parameters would be related to color. He would then scan the two sets of sixty leaves and feed the resulting data into software that would process them thanks to highly complex mathematical formulae. "The answer to your question," he said, "will be yes or no. It's a bit like putting the roses through a security system: the alarm goes on or doesn't. Give me a few days' time."

I waited for the results with trepidation, knowing I would feel like a fool if it turned out that my rose was nothing but a common 'Old Blush'. The following week, Mancuso called. "The two roses are clearly different," he said to my relief. "One is an 'Old Blush', and the other one is not. That's all I can say at this point."

It was all I had to know: De Rocco had been right after all. I thought I'd leave it at that, but it was not to be the last of my "De Rocco moments."

After the chance discovery of Lucia's Parisian diary, I found a large cache of her letters in the archives and became so absorbed by the life of my adventurous ancestress that I devoted a full-length biography to her. At the end of the book, I wrote that nothing much remained of Lucia's world today except a lovely pink rose that grew wild in the old park of Alvisopoli. Shortly after the book was published, I was invited to give a talk at the Circolo Società Casino Pedrocchi, a venerable old club in Padua. Afterward, I had a couple of hours to spare before taking the train back to Venice, so I wandered over to the Botanical Garden, one of Padua's attractions.

It is the oldest garden of its kind in Europe. The Benedictine monks of the Church of Santa Giustina founded it as early as 1545, after the Venetian Republic approved the establishment of a *Hortus officinalis* for medicinal plants. (Padua, in those days, served as Venice's university campus.) It is said that Daniele Barbaro, a Venetian statesman and an admirer of the Roman architect and engineer Vitruvius, designed the perfectly geometrical layout: a square inside a circle, with the square in turn divided into four smaller squares, or quarters.

Soon the monks were taking in all manner of exotic, highly coveted plants that Venetian merchants were bringing back from their long sea journeys. By 1552 a circular brick wall had to be erected around the garden to prevent night burglars from stealing precious species. Five centuries later the structure and layout have not changed. And the all-embracing wall, in addition to giving the garden its very distinct appearance, creates a warmly enveloping atmosphere.

It was the end of September when I ambled through the main gate. The plants, though fatigued after the long, hot summer, were giving out their last glorious flourish for the pleasure of late-season visitors like me. I walked down the short alley of rhododendrons, azaleas, and camellias, then turned toward the water lily pond and then to the old plots of medicinal herbs, poking warily around the poisonous and the carnivorous plants. I made my way from one quarter to the next, in a counterclockwise fashion, until, having gone full circle, I found myself in the northeast quarter staring at the oldest *Magnolia grandiflora* I had ever seen. A plaque said the tree had been planted in 1786. It was the same year Goethe visited the garden—also in late September. On his way to Venice he'd stopped in Padua to see the university, which he had found cramped and claustrophobic; he thought the Botanical Garden "much more cheerful." It occurred to me the garden could not have looked much different back then. In fact, some of the plants that had been growing in Goethe's time were still there, including a huge *Gingko biloba* from China planted in 1750, which now dominated the northwest quarter.

As I sat on a marble bench by the old magnolia, I pictured Goethe, tall and robust at thirty-seven, in his frock coat and breeches and mud-splattered buckled shoes, pausing here and there along the pathways to carefully observe each species. "What is seeing without thinking?" he had jotted down in his diary after spending several very profitable hours in the garden. For some time, he had been working on the idea that all species came from one original "primal plant." By his own admission he had "reached an impasse" in his theory, but his visit to the Botanical Garden in Padua unlocked his thinking.

The epiphany came when he found himself face-to-face with one of the oldest plants in the garden, a fan palm (*Chamaerops humilis*), acquired as early as 1585. He noticed how the young leaves at the base of the plant were full, like the tip of a lance, but then, as they grew, they started splitting and splaying like the fingers of a hand. He begged a reluctant gardener to cut him a few samples, which he eventually took back to Germany. In his studio in Weimar those samples became "fetishes that aroused and held my attention until I was able to foresee the happy results of my workings." In 1790, four years after his stop in Padua, Goethe published *The Metamorphosis of Plants*. For a long time, the scientific community dismissed his theory of the primal plant as the fanciful musings of a poet. But when I asked Mancuso about Goethe's theory, he told me that today many scientists have come to accept the theory's underlying premise. "In a way it is an application *ante litteram* of Darwin's evolutionary principle," he said.

The palm that inspired Goethe is still exactly where it was back in 1787, only now it is known as La Palma di Goethe. It is enclosed in a thirty-foot-high octagonal greenhouse, built in 1935—a mini skyscraper of glass

and steel designed in the rationalist style typical of Fascist architecture.

After leaving the greenhouse, I headed toward the fountain at the center of the garden, where the four paths intersect, intending to pause awhile in order to take in a 360-degree view of the garden before heading to the railway station. But the sight of a tall shrub ten yards away gave me a start. It was covered with pink roses that shimmered in the late morning sun. I slowed down deliberately so as not to shatter the spell, but as the rosebush came gradually into focus, I felt a second rush of adrenaline, for I was now certain, even before reaching the large shrub, that a familiar raspberry-scented fragrance was about to envelop me.

There was no tag attached, although all the other

plants seemed to have one. I asked a gardener, on all fours in a flower bed nearby, if he knew the name of the plant. He shook his head. "It's a China rose of some kind," he said. "But no one seems to know who planted it or how long it has been there. It must be pretty old."

The location was unusual. There were no other roses in the vicinity. The bulging shrub was squeezed between a bed of medicinal plants and the railing along the pathway. No one could possibly have planned to put it there.

Back in Venice, I wrote to the Botanical Garden to find out more about the rosebush, but the reply was not encouraging:

Dear Mr. Andrea di Robilant,

The rose about which you would like to have some information is, as far as we know, an **R. chinensis** *'Old Blush'. This is all the information we can give you since there is no archival record about the provenance or the date of acquisition for most plants.*

The passing note of hesitancy—*as far as we know*—evidently explained the absence of a tag. But I had no doubt: what the Botanical Garden thought was an 'Old

Blush' I knew to be a Rosa Moceniga. The question in my mind was: Who had put it there?

On a hunch, I called De Rocco's widow, Costanza, and asked her if she knew of any dealings her husband might have had with the Botanical Garden of Padua. She confirmed that he had indeed contacted them years earlier, in connection with the Rosa Moceniga, but as far as she could remember, he had been disappointed by the lack of interest. There seemed to be only one possible explanation: De Rocco, the compulsive rose planter, had surreptitiously placed the rose there.

Goethe was a compulsive planter as well. On his Italian journey, he collected plants that caught his fancy and often placed them in the gardens of friends he stayed with along the way. He said it was a way of leaving "a living memory" behind. I liked to think De Rocco had secretly left a living memory of his own. I imagined him waiting about in the garden until nearly closing time, the light fading until he was an indistinct shadow in the gloaming, then pulling out a cutting of his beloved rose and sticking it into the ground in that same narrow bed by the pathway where it stood now, fully grown.

Goethe, I am sure, would have been delighted by De Rocco's little piece of botanical mischief.

CHAPTER FOUR

Cordovado

Shortly after the book on Lucia came out, I received a call from my friend Benedetta Piccolomini, who has a rose garden in Cordovado, a small town built inside the ruins of a Roman military encampment, about four miles up the road from Alvisopoli.

"The story of your ancestor has created quite a stir among my rose friends," Benedetta said. "Signora Garlant would like to meet you. It's about your Rosa Moceniga."

Eleonora Garlant was known in the region as *la signora delle rose,* "the lady of the roses." She lived in Artegna, a medieval village at the foot of the Carnic Alps, where she had assembled, with the assistance of her husband, Valentino Fabiani, one of the largest collections of old roses in Italy. Although she was entirely self-taught, her knowledge in this field was said to be prodigious. Amateur rose collectors as well as professional horticulturists sought her out. Those who had visited her in Artegna claimed she had created such a rose-friendly environment that fabulous new hybrids grew spontaneously in her garden every year.

Signora Garlant was known in particular for her ability to identify long-lost roses from the past. De Rocco once told me he had driven up to see her with a potted Rosa Moceniga and left it with her in the hope that she might help him figure out what it was. So I was curious to hear what she had to say.

Benedetta suggested we meet at Alvisopoli, and a date was fixed. Our plan was to get the keys from Benito, the porter, and go look for the rose in the woods. On the appointed day, the weather was miserable. I stopped for gas on the way up to Alvisopoli and got out of the car under pelting rain. Blinded by the wind and the water streaming down my face, I unhooked the wrong hose and filled my diesel tank with unleaded gas. It took two hours to siphon the gas out with a makeshift suction device and fill it again with the proper fuel. Meanwhile, Benedetta called to say they were wet and tired of waiting, and it was getting dark. She asked if I would join them later at her house.

It was still pouring when I drove into Cordovado late in the evening. I had never been there before, but I knew something about the town from Lucia's letters and diaries. She had lived there in the 1790s, when her husband, Alvise, was reclaiming marshes and laying the foundations of what later became Alvisopoli. In those pioneering years, the swamps on which they built their utopian experiment were so malarial that they settled temporarily up the road, in a semi-abandoned country house in Cordovado, where the land was drier and the air cleaner.

In her diaries, a disheartened Lucia had written that she found the house in shambles, filled with dust and cobwebs and "completely useless" appliances. Everything had to be replaced: the old stove, the water tank,

the laundry basin, the casseroles and pans—not to mention the caretaker, an old drunk who resented the sudden invasion.

Images of Lucia's life in Cordovado came back to me as I drove by the old house she had lived in, straining to see through the windshield, which had misted over. Despite the scarce visibility, I caught a glimpse of the Mocenigo family crest above the main entrance (two roses, as it happened: a light blue rose against a white background in the upper half, and a white rose against a light blue background in the lower half).

I turned into the alley that led to the Piccolomini estate, which was spread out in the center of the town and surrounded by high walls. Nine Piccolomini brothers and sisters lived on the property, each with his or her separate house. Benedetta lived in one of the smaller ones. She was waiting for me at the door when I arrived. "Where on earth have you been?" she asked in mock reprimand as she hurried me into the living room.

Eleonora Garlant was sitting by the fireplace. She was in her early seventies, with soft, round features, thick glasses, and a warm smile that was highlighted with fuchsia lipstick. Her husband, Valentino, sat next to her. He was dressed in a Sunday suit and wore a dark tie. He had an angular profile, the nose of a boxer, and big, strong-looking hands.

Signora Garlant did most of the talking. She was excited by the connection between Lucia and Empress Josephine, and spoke with familiarity about the world of rose breeders who gravitated around Malmaison and the Jardin des Plantes. But she was especially curious about an episode that I had culled from Lucia's Paris diary concerning a rose long thought to be extinct.

In the entry for July 23, 1814, Lucia reported visiting Noisette's nursery on rue Saint-Jacques in the company of Joseph Martin, an expert gardener and adventurous rose chaser who worked under André Thouin at the Jardin des Plantes. Martin was a veteran of botanical expeditions to Madagascar, South Africa, the West Indies, and Latin America. In 1804 a British privateer captured his returning ship; he was imprisoned, and his valuable herbarium sold at auction. Martin was eventually repatriated and was now back on the job, helping out Lucia. Noisette showed them a cultivar they called "Rose Bichonne." As they took turns smelling this exotic specimen that had recently arrived from China, a discussion developed about its fragrance. Lucia thought it definitely smelled of peaches, but Monsieur Martin and Monsieur Noisette had different opinions: one of them (she does not say which) argued in favor of pineapple, while the other insisted it smelled of raspberry gelée.

When I had first come across this amusing sniffing contest in Lucia's diary, it occurred to me that a combination of peach, pineapple, and raspberry gelée described very well the rich scent of the Rosa Moceniga—at least according to my nose. Signora Garlant agreed, adding that she detected "a touch of cinnamon" as well. In fact, she had been so overwhelmed by the fruity fragrance of the Rosa Moceniga back when De Rocco brought her a small plant that she had sensed right away it could not possibly be the bland-scented 'Old Blush'.

Now she wondered whether the Rosa Moceniga might not be the long-lost Rose Bichonne described by

Lucia. Eagerly, we pulled out from Benedetta's well-furnished library an edition of *Les roses*, Pierre-Joseph Redouté's masterly collection of color drawings published in the 1820s, which depicts the roses known in Josephine's time. And there it was: a splendidly rendered Rose Bichonne. However, it was not the color we hoped it would be. While similar in many aspects to the Rosa Moceniga—the leaves, the shape of the flower, the number of petals, the thorns—the Rose Bichonne painted by Redouté was crimson, not pink. Apparently, it was not the Rosa Moceniga after all. There was, however, an element of confusion. On the left side, under the drawing, was the Latin name *R. indica;* on the right side was the French name Rose Bichonne. *R. indica* is the pink Chinese reflowering rose that Pehr Osbeck, Linnaeus's assistant, brought back from Canton in the 1750s. Linnaeus had his own specimen plant of *R. indica,* which he called Blush Tea China. But the crimson rose painted by Redouté was nothing like the blush-colored rose Linnaeus called *R. indica*.

It was hard to imagine that Redouté, a considerable rose expert himself, would have used the wrong color to paint the Rose Bichonne. Still, there was enough uncertainty about the matter that I was not quite ready to let go of my raspberry-scented clue.

Nor was Signora Garlant. "We must write to Monsieur Joyaux," she said solemnly as our party disbanded.

The name meant nothing to me at the time, but I soon learned that François Joyaux was regarded as a great authority on old roses. Gallicas were his field of expertise: in his garden at Commer, in the Pays de la Loire region, he grew every known form and variety of this particular rose—three hundred in all. It was a *collection nationale*, a national treasure.

I later asked Signora Garlant why she did not think of seeking the advice of contemporary rose breeders such as Peter Beales or David Austin, names even I was familiar with. She replied rather haughtily that they were "tradesmen," meaning by this, I suppose, that the business of selling roses on a very large scale must surely affect the quality of their judgment. Joyaux, on the other hand, was a "true maestro," a rose collector both passionate and rigorous. Furthermore, he had written extensively about Empress Josephine's collection at Malmaison and was very familiar with the world of Professor Desfontaines, the chief gardener Monsieur Thouin, the *serviteur des roses* Monsieur Du Pont, and of course Louis Noisette, the nurseryman. Hence the man to ask.

Signora Garlant did not speak a word of French, so

she enlisted her neighbor Ms. Liliana Berini, who had studied the language in the town school, to help her compose a letter to Joyaux, a copy of which she later sent to me (my translation).

Dear Monsieur Joyaux,

I have recently obtained a rose that we call Rosa Moceniga here in my parts but that might in fact be a Rose Bichonne. It looks very much like an 'Old Blush': the flower is similar (5 to 7 cm in diameter, 16–18 petals) and so is the color, light pink in the center and darker around the edges. The prickles, like those of the 'Old Blush', are opaque and sparse. But the leaves are darker, more pointed, and not as shiny. And it carries itself better than the 'Old Blush'. The limbs are thin and tend to arch. It smells of peaches, pineapple, raspberry, and cinnamon and reflowers frequently. It grows wild in the nearby woods of Alvisopoli, the estate that once belonged to the Mocenigos, a Venetian family that gave many doges to the Republic.

This particular rose tends to colonize the space around it. There were several shrubs scattered around at some distance one from the other when I last saw it in the woods. Apparently a Venetian dame by the name of Lucia Mocenigo brought it from Paris in 1814. She knew Empress Josephine and often called on her at Malmaison. She studied with Monsieur Du Pont, the serviteur des roses *at the Jardin des Plantes—a good-natured man who had a collection of 400 roses and taught Lucia the art of grafting. She brought back seeds and plants, which she purchased at Monsieur Noisette's nursery on rue Saint-Jacques. The Rosa Moceniga was probably among these. I draw this information from* Lucia: A Venetian Life in the Age of Napoleon, *written by Andrea di Robilant, a descendant of Lucia Mocenigo.*

Does all this make sense, and might this rose actually be a Rose Bichonne? Given your experience, vast knowledge, and easy access to old books and catalogs, I hope you will be able to answer my question and satisfy my curiosity.

I am attaching a photograph of the Rosa Moceniga. Thank you for reading my letter.

Yours,
Eleonora Garlant

I was skeptical: Joyaux probably received hundreds of these letters every year. But Signora Garlant was confident of a reply: he did not know her, this much she conceded, but she was, after all, a member of Rosa Gallica, the nonprofit organization that Joyaux had founded, and a subscriber to its bimonthly bulletin (which the trusty Ms. Berini translated for her).

A year went by, and I heard nothing more on the matter. One day Benedetta called me to say she was organizing a two-day gathering of gardeners and horticulturists at Cordovado. Would I come to say a few words about Lucia and the Rosa Moceniga? My ignorance about roses should have been reason enough to decline, but I found myself accepting the invitation because Signora Garlant was going to attend and I was hoping to revive our lagging chase for the Rosa Moceniga. Days later, I received in the mail a brochure for the event. It said that I would be giving a talk about *una rosa misteriosa*—"a mysterious rose." I felt like an impostor about to be found out.

On the day of the meeting the weather was fine and the garden looked glorious. Ramblers and climbers and shrubs were in full bloom. Visitors walked around the grounds taking pictures and admiring Benedetta's roses. I noticed Signora Garlant in the crowd and went over to say hello.

I asked her if she had heard back from Joyaux.

"I just received this letter," she said, grinning, and pulled out an envelope from her bag. Joyaux's reply to her was written on fine French stationery, under a rather intimidating letterhead:

ROSERAIE DE LA COUR DE COMMER;

CONSERVATOIRE DE VARIÉTÉS HORTICOLES RARES;

COLLECTION NATIONALE DE ROSES GALLIQUES.

Madame,

I received your letter about the Rosa Moceniga. Please accept my apology for being so tardy in responding to you. The reason is quite simple. I tried hard to provide an answer to your question, but finding nothing in my personal archives, I had to wait until I visited the Museum of Natural History in Paris to pursue my research. Time went by. Forgive me.

What you tell me about this Lucia Mocenigo is extremely interesting. As you perhaps know, I have written a book on the roses of Empress Josephine—so you can well imagine how the topic fascinates me. Unfortunately my research on your behalf has produced very meager results . . .

Joyaux confirmed that there did once exist, among the roses of China, a Rose Bichonne. According to the *Rosetum gallicum* of Narcisse Desportes, it had several synonyms: "rose bichon," "bengale guenille," "bengale pourpre panachée," "bengale à odeur de cannelle," "bengale à odeur de capucine," *"rosa pannosa,"* and *"rosa sinica pannosa."*

> ... But in the **Rosetum gallicum** *it says that this Rose Bichonne was a variegated purple, and therefore not like the rose I see in the picture you sent to me. In conclusion, the Rosa Moceniga probably corresponds to a variety other than the Rose Bichonne. I imagine this will disappoint you. But if you have nothing against it, I will use the information about Lucia and the roses to write an article for the next issue of* **Rosa Gallica.** *Perhaps a reader will come up with a better answer than mine. And by the way, if you should learn more about Lucia's stay in Paris and her friendship with Empress Josephine I would be very pleased if you shared it with me.*
>
> *Please accept my best wishes,*
> *François Joyaux*

Despite Joyaux's "meager results," I could see that Signora Garlant was thrilled to have excited the great man's curiosity. Meanwhile, the time had come to give my dreaded talk on *la rosa misteriosa*. Fortunately, Benedetta had arranged to have Signora Garlant on the podium with me. After a few perfunctory remarks on my part, she came to my rescue and took over the conversation, to the delight of the audience and me.

Later, I thanked her for making it easy.

"It is all Lucia's doing," she replied, smiling.

A few days later I received a copy of her reply to Joyaux. I could not help but notice how her tone, expertly conveyed by Ms. Berini, the translator, had grown increasingly self-confident:

To the attention of Monsieur Joyaux

I am happy to learn that you are greatly interested in Lucia Mocenigo and her friendship with Empress Josephine. I am taking the liberty of sending along a copy of Andrea di Robilant's Lucia: A Venetian Life in the Age of Napoleon.

In chapter 9 you will find all the information
concerning Lucia's sojourn in Paris and her
friendship with Josephine.

I have asked the author, whom I know
personally, to write to you directly, and I am
including his letter in this package.

I look forward to reading your article on Lucia
and the Rosa Moceniga in your next bulletin.

My best wishes,
Eleonora Garlant

Although I was wary of being drawn into a correspondence between rose experts, it seemed to me
unkind to go against Signora Garlant's wishes. Here is
an excerpt from my letter:

Dear Monsieur Joyaux,

Madame Eleonora Garlant has told me about
your interest in my great-great-great-great-
grandmother, her friendship with Empress
Josephine, and the plants she brought back from
Paris after the fall of Napoleon . . . As you shall
see, at the end of my book I write that nothing

remains of Lucia's garden at Alvisopoli except for
a beautiful rose, very fragrant, that grows wild
among the ruins of the old park. The local folk
call it Rosa Moceniga but do not know its origin.
It is very likely it was among the roses Lucia
brought back from Paris . . .

*n*early a year went by with no reply. Then one day
Signora Garlant received a parcel containing two
letters and a book. It turned out Joyaux had not been
well. He was now much better and apologized for his
long silence.

One letter was addressed to Signora Garlant:

Chère Madame,

You will find it very surprising and ill-mannered
to be receiving an answer ten months after your
letter. But I've had to interrupt all activity since
last June. I am only now getting back to work,
and I was especially keen to begin by renewing
my correspondence with you . . .

Drawing from your letters and Andrea di

Robilant's book on Lucia, I have written a little essay that will appear in no. 62 of **Rosa Gallica** *next July. I hope you will like it. You will receive no. 61 in the next few days.*

This long silence is really quite unforgivable. And yet I dare ask you: if by any chance you were able to obtain a cutting of Rosa Moceniga, I would love to have one so as to place it in our collection here at Commer.

Again, forgive my long silence. And please accept my most respectful consideration.

François Joyaux

The second letter was to me:

Monsieur,

Like Madame Garlant, you, too, will be quite surprised to receive such a belated reply to your letter. I hope you will forgive my rudeness . . . I found the book very interesting. Of course I was especially keen to read the chapter on Lucia and Empress Josephine. I hope you will find the text I have written for our bulletin suitable.

Some years back I wrote a book about Josephine and her roses—Les roses de l'impératrice: La rosomanie au temps de Joséphine. *The book is alas out of print, and I cannot send you a copy. Had I known about the Rosa Moceniga, there is no doubt I would have devoted an additional chapter to it. I am sending you another book,* La rose: Une passion française, *in which you will find several pages on the topic of Josephine and her roses.*

François Joyaux

Issue number 62 of the bulletin *Rosa Gallica* was, as Joyaux had promised, largely devoted to Lucia and the Rosa Moceniga. Signora Garlant e-mailed Joyaux:

I am happy to see that this rose has generated so much interest. It will be my special care, in the autumn, to send you a Rosa Moceniga in a pot so that it will already have its roots. I am really quite thrilled at the idea that my plant will be in your garden.

Please accept my deepest thanks and most cordial salutations.

*I*n late November Signora Garlant called to tell me that a potted Rosa Moceniga was on its way to France by courier. "She is making her return journey two hundred years after Lucia brought her here," she announced.

Joyaux e-mailed back at the end of December wishing Signora Garlant a happy New Year. "The rose has arrived," he added. "All is well."

In April, word came from Joyaux that the first roses had bloomed on the little shrub at Commer.

CHAPTER FIVE

Eleonora's Old Roses

The road to Artegna passes through cornfields and vineyards and then climbs gently into the hills of northeastern Friuli. In the middle distance, the rugged Carnic Alps hang like a dark gray curtain separating this region from Slovenia.

Eleonora—Signora Garlant and I were now on a first-name basis—had called me a few weeks earlier to say that a new rose was about to bloom: the latest addition to her large family of natural hybrids. "I am going to call it Lucia, in honor of your ancestor," she said. "You should come up for the christening. We'll open a bottle of wine."

I welcomed the idea of driving through the open countryside of Friuli, with its rolling farmlands and quiet little towns. The region once served as the main passage between Italy and Central Europe. Hungarians, Huns, Ostrogoths, Lombards, Franks, and Germans— all came through at different times before the Venetians took over in the fifteenth century.

As a result, the Friulani are an unusual mix of Italian, Germanic, and Slav cultures: proud, independent, hardworking, and deeply attached to the land. They speak their own language—a version of Romansch—and call Friuli the Little Fatherland.

My first trip to Friuli was in 1976. I had driven up in the aftermath of a devastating earthquake, to help out as a volunteer. The spirit of the Friulani impressed us students who had taken leave from college to come lend a hand. Undaunted by the devastation all around them, the residents took care of their dead and wounded and got on with their lives, clearing the rubble, helping one another out, never fussing or complaining. And at the end of each day, they still had time to pass around a big bottle of Merlot before taking cover for the night in makeshift shelters. *"Fasin di besoi,"* they used to say in their dialect. "We manage on our own."

On the way to Eleonora's, I recognized the names of towns and villages that had been flattened by the earthquake more than thirty years earlier and now were back on their feet, steadfast and thriving across the Little Fatherland.

The road wound through Artegna and came to a dead end in a dusty parking lot next to a construction site—a new sports facility, by the look of it. "Our house is the last one before the railroad tracks," Eleonora had said over the phone. I rang the buzzer, the green metal gate opened with a whirr, and she appeared in the alleyway, flashing her signature fuchsia smile, while Valentino followed behind her.

They lived in an unassuming one-story detached house, which they had built in the early 1970s on a little less than two acres of land. A few years after moving in, Eleonora told Valentino she was keen to plant some roses in her garden. Conveniently, the thirtieth anniversary of their wedding was coming up. "I asked my husband to give me an *old* rose," she said, leading me into the garden. "I had to press the point, because he wouldn't have known the difference."

My heart went out to Valentino, because I, too, was finding it difficult to distinguish an old rose from a modern one—especially those bred to look like old ones! The difference has always been a matter of some controversy. Until recently most rose breeders and collectors generally accepted 1867 as the dividing mark. That was the year Jean-Baptiste Guillot, a nurseryman in Lyon, found in one of his patches a rose that was different from any seen before. It was the product of a natural liaison between one of his hybrid perpetuals and one of his teas, and it became the first of a new and fast-growing family called the hybrid teas. Guillot proudly named it 'La France', and despite the early resistance of British breeders, it was long regarded as the first of the modern roses. But many breeders and collectors—and not just in Britain—began to feel that such an early cutoff point was arbitrary and misleading. Finally, at the World Rose Convention held in Vancouver in 2009, the great divide between old and modern roses was officially moved up to 1900.

Many believe, and Eleonora is among them, that even some roses produced after 1900 have the appearance and feel and scent of old roses. "Just look at the rose and don't bother with dates," she suggested to me. "Old roses fall naturally, have a richer fragrance, and usually come in soft, delicate shades. Modern roses are like little soldiers standing at attention. The stems shoot straight up, the petals are rigid, the colors are sharp: frankly, they look as though they've had work done on them."

In any event, Valentino surprised Eleonora on the day of their wedding anniversary by giving her not one but thirty different old roses—one for each year of their marriage.

"That is how it all started," she said. "I never grew a modern rose again."

"I should have bought you a necklace," Valentino mumbled in the background.

The thirty roses quickly filled out the space in front of the house. So Eleonora had Valentino clear the field behind the house and prepare a large rectangular vegetable patch, around which she planted more roses. Soon she was ordering and collecting new varieties at a pace Valentino struggled to keep up with. He dug up another vegetable patch, and then another. And around these he built pergolas with strong poles made of chestnut, so Eleonora could place her roses around the perimeter, as her mother had taught her to do when she was a little girl.

"I guess the garden just designed itself over time," Eleonora told me, adding that she had never so much as sketched a layout on a notepad. "I planted roses, mixing climbers and shrubs in a way that made sense to me. I aimed for color combinations that were harmonious and pleasing. That's all. I can't say I was inspired by other gardens or that I tried to replicate effects seen elsewhere. I had never seen a formal rose garden before starting this one."

I asked Eleonora how many rose species and varieties she had in her garden. "One thousand four hundred and eighty-five," she answered very precisely, "and the number keeps growing." One thousand four hundred and eighty-five! It seemed to me like an awful lot of roses for the two of them to take care of—and it is. Eleonora and Valentino work long hours every day all year round. The routine can be grueling, especially in early spring, when it is hard to keep the garden under control. Yet they stubbornly refuse outside help. *Fasin di besoi* is their motto.

The three vegetable patches, which form the heart of the garden, are roughly of equal size, rectangular in shape (twenty-five by seventy-five feet), set one after the other along the same axis. When standing inside them, one has the impression of entering a suite of three beautiful rooms, each one enclosed by curtains of cascading clusters of white-pink roses of all sizes and shapes.

Eleonora walked me through these rooms, indicating each rose by name and telling me where it had come from and, if it was named after a person, the story of its namesake. Occasionally, she'd stop to hold a rose in her two hands and, addressing the flower directly, inquire about a blemished petal or a curling leaf. Did it need more sunshine? Had it soaked up too much water during the last rainfall? There was nothing condescending in her manner of speaking; she didn't baby-talk or humor the rose. She was after specific information.

Valentino, who had planted every single one of the roses in his wife's garden, followed at a distance. I tried to draw him into the conversation, but every time I asked him about this or that rose, he demurred. "I know nothing," he said. "She tells me where to dig, and I dig. She tells me where to plant, and I plant." But he was not entirely convincing.

Beyond the three vegetable patches, the garden became informal and romantic. Different varieties of Albas, Damasks, and Gallicas climbed up trees, tumbled down from rough-hewn pergolas, or surged from the ground in a heavenly profusion of colors and scents. These great aristocratic roses seemed to have found a home where they could unleash their energy and proliferate with abandon.

Deeper into this part of the garden, Eleonora had planted exotic roses from as far away as Chile and Tibet. And beyond those, in a separate section, she kept her "recovered roses"—varieties that had strayed or were thought to have died out and that she had found over the years in abandoned gardens, in cemeteries, and among the ruins of old villas and castles. Most of these were still unidentified, and she'd named them, temporarily, after the place where they came from or the person who found them.

Scattered around the property were sixty or so natural hybrids that had come to life spontaneously in Eleonora's garden—the result of secretive affairs between her roses. She did not know who the parent roses were, nor did she seem particularly interested. The new hybrid we were about to christen Lucia belonged to this group.

On the way back to the house, we returned through the suite of vegetable gardens, which Valentino kept very neat and clear of weeds. The first one was lined with rows of arugula, Swiss chard, various types of lettuce, and the light green and tender *radicchio di Trieste*—a local delicacy quite different from the better-known red and bitter *radicchio di Treviso*. Along the perimeter, roses fell from the chestnut pergolas like shimmering white-pink curtains. There were no tags, so

I had trouble identifying the different cultivars. I recognized some of the better-known varieties—the very light 'Souvenir de la Malmaison', which reminded me of white peaches; the pale pink 'Belle Portugaise'; and the sweet-scented 'Mme Alfred Carrière', with its creamy-white soft, loose petals. But there was such an overflow of roses, such a profusion of colors and fragrances, that in a moment everything around me became a jumble.

Eleonora came to my rescue, bringing order to the dizzying beauty around me. She pointed out an 'Empress Josephine' spread languidly against a corner post of the pergola, showing off its reddish-pink roses. "Empress Josephine!" I repeated, heading toward it the way one gravitates toward a familiar face in a crowded drawing room

The breeders in Josephine's time started the fashion of giving roses evocative names to entice clients or simply to curry favor—before then, roses were known only by their Latin names. At Malmaison, for example, *R. alba incarnata* famously became 'Cuisse de Nymphe Émue', or "Thigh of a Deeply Moved Nymph." Not all names were so extravagant. They usually described the color of the rose: 'Belle Pourpre Violette', 'Cramoisi Éblouissant' ("Beautiful Violet Purple" and "Dazzling Crimson," respectively). In some cases, rose names were inspired by antiquity, as with 'Belle Hélène', or "Beautiful Helen." It was only after the fall of the empire, during the Restoration, that it became chic to have a rose named after oneself. In fact, so many people in high places wanted a rose named for them that there were not enough roses to go around. The total number of roses was still only in the hundreds during the earlier part of the nineteenth century, before the impact of the Chinese studs, so a rose was often given several names, and these were called synonyms.

Naming a rose after a person creates an indissoluble association. When I saw the 'Empress Josephine' spread out against Eleonora's corner pergola, I inevitably conjured up the real Josephine. And so it was with the other roses arrayed around it. I was no longer simply walking along a path looking at the roses on display. I had stepped into a crowded, lively room filled with roses that were looking at me.

Next to the 'Empress Josephine' was a beautiful pink climber. "'Duchesse de Montebello'," Eleonora said, cupping her hands around one of its flowers. The real Duchess of Montebello, she explained, was Louise Ghéhéneuc, the pretty young widow of Maréchal Jean Lannes, one of Napoleon's most trusted generals. He received the title of Duke of Montebello for his bravery in the Second Italian Campaign. He and the duchess had been one of the rising couples at the emperor's court. But Lannes died of his wounds on the battlefield at Esslingen, in May 1809, and a distraught Napoleon wrote to Josephine asking her to console "the poor

Duchesse de Montebello

Duchess." A year later, after divorcing Josephine, Napoleon named Louise lady-in-waiting to the new empress, Marie Louise—hardly a consolation for "the poor Duchess," who nevertheless managed to remain a close friend of Josephine's.

"I have put them next to each other," Eleonora said of the roses named after the two friends. "They keep each other company."

Nearby was a 'Baltimore Belle', a late-flowering pale pink climber that belonged to the same period. It was named after Betsy Patterson, the American wife of Napoleon's youngest brother, the unruly Jérôme Bonaparte.

I've always found it impossible to keep track of Napoleon's many siblings, but Jérôme is easy: he's the one who married the American, and I knew their story well. Napoleon had little patience with his youngest brother and sent him off to the navy to straighten him out. Once in the Antilles, Jérôme jumped ship, landed in the United States, and lived in style by mooching off the French chargé d'affaires. He fell in love with Elizabeth Patterson, the pretty daughter of a rich Baltimore merchant, and proposed to her. He was nineteen; she was eighteen. Mr. Patterson tried to get in the way, but Betsy, as she was known, stood her ground, famously telling her father that she would rather be Jérôme's for an hour than another man's for a lifetime. They married on Christmas Eve 1803. Napoleon blocked all funds and ordered his brother to come home—without his wife. Worried about his future inheritance now that Napoleon was about to be crowned emperor, Jérôme sailed to France with a pregnant Betsy, hoping to mollify his older brother. But when they arrived in Lisbon, only

Jérôme's passport was waiting for them. They continued to Amsterdam, but still Betsy was not allowed to disembark. She finally headed to England, where she gave birth to their child, while Jérôme went to Paris. His manipulative older brother welcomed him back

Baltimore Belle

into the family fold, forced him to marry Catherine of Württemberg, and crowned him King of Westphalia.[*]

---

[*] Catherine, who had a beautiful garden at Schloss Wilhelmshöhe, near Kassel, brought Jérôme even deeper into the world of roses. She and Josephine corresponded regularly and exchanged many roses. Catherine had the court painter, Salomon Pinhas, paint the roses in her garden, much like Redouté had done at Malmaison. The paintings hang in the library at Wilhelmshöhe. It is said that

Elizabeth never saw Jérôme again. She returned to Baltimore with her son, Jérôme Napoleon Bonaparte, known as Bo.

Betsy was still alive in 1843 (she died in 1879, at the age of ninety-four), when a Baltimore nurseryman, Samuel Feast, crossed a Gallica hybrid with an American prairie rose (*R. setigera*) to produce a lovely pink climber he called 'Baltimore Belle'. Curiously, the same year, a French nurseryman, Monsieur Robert, introduced a rose he named 'Catherine de Württemberg'. It is a darker pink than 'Baltimore Belle', and not as pretty or as fragrant. I asked Eleonora if she had a 'Catherine de Württemberg' in her garden. She shook her head and chuckled. "I've always been on Betsy's side."

Before moving on, Eleonora pulled out a kitchen knife, stepped into the vegetable patch, and cut several heads of *radicchio di Trieste*. "I'll put these in a bag for you. You will like them. The leaves are very tender."

In the second vegetable garden, Valentino had planted, under Eleonora's precise instructions, string beans, tomatoes, eggplant, zucchini, and red and yellow peppers. It was still early in the season, and the plants were no more than six to eight inches high, all lined up

---

Catherine's gardener, Daniel August Schwartzkopf, hybridized the first German rose cultivar, 'Perle von Weissenstein'.

neatly in their furrows; they looked comfortably settled into the soil, ready to burst with the first summer sunshine. "In just a few weeks," Eleonora said, "touches of bright red and yellow and purple will be showing in between the fresh green leaves."

Along the pergola-covered path that ran around the vegetable patch, roses tumbled forth like pink waterfalls. I recognized some of the more popular varieties: the very light and fragrant 'Fantin-Latour', the light pink 'Mme d'Arblay', the rosy-white 'Champneys' Pink Cluster' (the first of the Noisettes). The dominant color here also was pink, but it was mixed with more vivid colors, such as the purple/russet of 'Archduke Joseph' or the egg-yolk yellow of 'Claire Jacquier'.

For a long time the roses in European gardens came mostly in shades of white and pink. Chinese roses introduced scarlet red only at the end of the eighteenth century. Yellow appeared much later, thanks to the French nurseryman Joseph Pernet-Ducher. For thirteen years he tried in vain to cross the deep yellow *R. foetida persiana,* which the British envoy Sir Henry Willcock had brought from Persia in 1837, with one of his hybrid teas. Then, one morning in 1900, he went to inspect his patch and noticed a hint of yellow in the new bloom that turned to light gold toward the center of the rose.

He called it 'Soleil d'Or', "Golden Sunshine." Ten years later, he introduced 'Rayon d'Or', "Golden Ray." These generated a group of yellow hybrid teas called Pernetianas.

"But Pernet-Ducher's best-known creation is over here," Eleonora said, leading me to a sturdy climber carrying large clusters of elegant, assertive, silky-pink roses.

"What is her name?" I asked.

"'Madame Caroline Testout'," Eleonora said with an admiration that seemed directed as much to the rose as to the person it was named after.

The real Madame Testout was a savvy fashion designer of the Belle Epoque, with showrooms in Paris and London. She used to purchase her silks in Lyon, which was also the center for the rose trade. Hybrid teas were all the rage then. In the years following Guillot's introduction of 'La France' in 1867, the busy nurserymen near Lyon developed more than one thousand new hybrids. Madame Testout thought it would be very good publicity for her business if a new rose were named after her. She went to see Pernet-Ducher, one of the ablest nurserymen in the region, and charmed him into developing a new hybrid and giving it her name. The gorgeous 'Mme Caroline Testout' duly made its appearance, and large bunches of it were soon filling the windows of Madame Testout's rooms at the spring fashion show of 1890. 'Mme Caroline Testout' became hugely popular all over Europe and in the United States. (Fifteen years later, in 1905, half a million shrubs were planted along the streets and avenues of Portland, Oregon, to mark the centennial of the Lewis and Clark Expedition.)

Caroline Testout

Pernet-Ducher was delighted by the success of the new rose. Not so his jealous wife. The poor man tried to placate her by breeding a rose just for her but ended by making matters worse. 'Mme Pernet-Ducher' turned out to be rather plain and was soon forgotten.

*I*n the third vegetable garden, the one farthest from the house, Valentino had planted only potatoes (under strict orders from Eleonora). The potato flowers were just then in bloom, and the patch had taken on the appearance of a lovely green bedspread decorated with white floral embroidery.

Upon entering the garden, I spotted the pink clusters of 'La France'—long considered the first "modern" rose—which I had seen many times in pictures. I remembered reading somewhere that Peter Beales thought the rose somewhat "inconspicuous," given the "heavy mantle" it carried. I understood what he meant, now that I was seeing it for the first time in a garden. The flowers were smallish, and the shrub was not very sturdy, whereas I had expected a rose with a grander disposition, given the demands of its name. But on second thought it occurred to me that the "heavy mantle" on those delicate limbs was perhaps what made it so endearing.

*E*leonora always thought choosing 'La France' as the dividing mark between old and modern roses had been arbitrary, "but it reminds you of the clout the

French had in the world of roses in the nineteenth century." She is not entirely satisfied with the new cutoff date either—1900—and believes World War I would have been a more sensible choice. "After the war, hybridization really kicked into high gear. Rosebuds became very popular, and nurseries started to mass-produce roses to feed the new fashion. Old roses went into rapid decline. If you look at the catalogs published after 1920, you see how they disappeared year after year. Nurseries couldn't sell them, so they stopped producing them. We lost hundreds, if not thousands, of varieties."

Eleonora led me to a beautiful climber with cupped flowers of a delicate sulphur-yellow hue. "We thought we had lost this one as well during that fateful period," she said, claiming it was a 'Parks' Yellow Tea-Scented China', one of the famous stud Chinas and the parent of many fine yellow teas. Traces of this historic variety had disappeared until the 1980s, when Peter Beales said he found a specimen hidden away in his nursery. "Sadly I have no recollection or record of whence or from whom it came," he wrote at the time. Despite Beales's claim, it is still generally accepted that Parks' Yellow is extinct, but I wondered if the rose had had a secret new life, and whether a splendid specimen was indeed stretched out in front of me.

I took a sniff and was surprised that it didn't really smell of tea at all.

This may have been because my sense of smell was being distracted by the inebriating fragrance of a rose-bush just a few steps away, one covered with pinkish white flowers that were packed with petals and slightly pressed.

"Ahhh, Mademoiselle de Sombreuil!" Eleonora suddenly declaimed, poised on the edge of the potato field like an operatic diva. "Drink up this glass of aristocratic blood or see your father die!"

Now it was 1792, the height of the Terror in revolutionary France. Charles François Virot, Marquess of Sombreuil and former governor of Les Invalides, the Parisian armory, was accused of harboring royalist sympathies and dragged to the crowded prison at the Abbaye de Saint-Germain-des-Prés. His young daughter, Marie-Maurille Virot de Sombreuil, refused to leave his side and followed him to jail. The marquess was eventually dragged to a makeshift tribunal. Mademoiselle de Sombreuil pleaded for his life, begging the executioner to take pity on her father in his old age. She asked to be killed in his place.

The executioner told her to show her good faith by drinking a glass of aristocratic blood. She gulped it down in one swill. The crowd roared, and she and her father were both set free.

"It turned out the executioner had given her a glass of red wine," Eleonora quipped. Two years later, the marquess was again arrested, but this time he did not escape the guillotine. The exceptionally fragrant white rose named after his daughter has become a symbol of filial piety.

I enjoyed listening to Eleonora's stories. Her notion of history was entirely shaped by these anecdotes. She knew dozens, possibly hundreds of wonderful rose stories that involved traveling monks, crusaders, merchants, eccentric collectors, famous French *grandes dames,* and crafty businesswomen such as Madame Testout. In a way, she had constructed in her mind a rose's history of the world, which she was happy to disclose in her enthusiastic manner.

Eleonora headed back to the house to prepare for the christening. I stayed among the roses, chasing colors and fragrances in a state of merry intoxication. Then I came upon a rose of extravagant sensuality bursting forth unabashedly in large, abundant clusters. The outer petals were a delicate light pink, very soft and languorous; toward the center of the flower the shade turned darker and more mysterious, and the petals curled ever so gently into thin cherry-colored lips.

I knew instantly it was a 'Jenny Duval,' for I had seen this very rose posing seductively in a photograph by Georges Lévêque published in François Joyaux's classic *La rose de France*. I leaned into the flower and shamelessly buried my face in it.

For a long time it was thought this rose was a cross between a Gallica and a Chinese rose introduced by Hippolyte Duval, a nineteenth-century nurseryman in Montmorency. But British rose experts argued that 'Jenny Duval' was exactly the same as 'Président de Sèze', a well-known cultivar introduced in 1836. So 'Jenny Duval' has faded into the background over the years. But when I later brought up the subject with Eleonora, she insisted that 'Jenny Duval' and 'Président de Sèze' were two different roses. "I have both in my garden," she told me, "and I can assure you they are not at all alike." Still, she could not tell me why the former was named 'Jenny Duval', and I never managed to get to the bottom of it. The only plausible explanation I read was that Duval, the nurseryman, may have named the rose Jenny for some personal reason. It then became known as Jenny de Duval—that is, "Jenny of Duval." Over time the genitive disappeared, and Jenny Duval became the actual name of the rose, even though there was no Jenny Duval. So it came to this: 'Jenny Duval' was a rose that many (across the Channel) thought did not exist, one that bore the name of a woman who also did not exist.

Yet there I stood, in Eleonora's potato patch, utterly enthralled by the decadent beauty of 'Jenny Duval'. Since there was no story attached to it—no real person on whom to fix my thoughts—I filled the void by conjuring up the only woman I knew with a similar name: Charles Baudelaire's legendary lover Jeanne Duval, a sultry Haitian-born beauty he called his Black Venus. The Impressionist artist Edouard Manet painted a remarkable portrait of Jeanne Duval sprawled on a divan, her dark features and black hair in stark contrast to the immense white dress she's wearing. In my imagination, I pinned a freshly cut mauve-pink 'Jenny Duval' to her hair—that same thick, luscious hair that inspired Baudelaire to write in a letter to the real Jeanne Duval:

*Let me breathe at length, at length the smell
of your hair, and bury my face in it like a man*

quenching his thirst at a spring, and shake it like
a sweet scented handkerchief to let memories free.

Eleonora's shrill voice shook me out of my reverie. All was ready for the christening. I ambled toward a clearing near the house where the newborn Lucia, a feisty rambler, was already stretching its limbs around a pergola's base. The little rose was a creamy white

Jenny Duval

semi-double, with pointed petals and a spicy scent that reminded me of cinnamon. Eleonora had invited a few friends over for the occasion. The sun was just then setting over the railroad tracks, and the garden was bathed in a warm golden light.

She cut the flower and put the stem into a small ampulla. Pictures were taken. Valentino uncorked a bottle with a loud pop, and we filled our glasses with sparkling Prosecco.

"To Lucia!" Eleonora toasted. "To Lucia!" we all happily replied.

CHAPTER SIX

The Bee and the Hawfinch

"ere's another one," Valentino cried out to Eleonora.

It was early spring. Nearly a year had passed since my first visit to Artegna, and I was back in Eleonora's garden taking notes for a magazine piece on natural rose hybrids. At the far end of the garden, Valentino had been clearing the ground of dead branches and rotten leaves, and he had spotted a seedling pushing through the winter debris.

Eleonora headed toward Valentino, and I followed in her footsteps.

If the new hybrid was growing in a shady area or one that was already crowded with roses, she was going to have him dig it out and place it in a pot. Once the plant was strong enough to be moved, Valentino would put it back into the ground in a more suitable spot. But it turned out the little rose was in a sunny clearing, protected by other rose shrubs yet far enough from them to have sufficient space and light to grow at its leisure.

"We can leave it here," Eleonora said. "It will do fine."

Every spring, when the ground has loosened and the garden comes sluggishly back to life, Valentino finds five or six new hybrids scattered around the property. He has developed a keen eye under his wife's tutelage. "I guess he has learned to distinguish a newborn rose from a bramble," Eleonora chuckled, as we walked away.

Although spontaneous hybridization between roses has always occurred in nature, it is not a common phenomenon, and when it does happen, usually no one is there to take note of it. In Eleonora's garden, however, natural hybrids thrive. At the time of my second visit, forty of them were already fully grown, while another twenty were on their way to producing their first blossom: sixty new roses that will only ever be seen in her garden. And every year, there are more.

The notion that plant diversity is rapidly diminishing on our planet is so ingrained in us that what occurs in Eleonora's garden takes on a magical aura. But there is no trick; it is nature at work. And these old roses have found such an idyllic breeding ground that apparently they cannot wait to get on with it.

One may argue, of course, that these hybrids are not old roses *sensu stricto,* since they are coming to life more than a century after the current dividing mark between old roses and modern roses (1900). But when I raised the issue with Eleonora, she simply shrugged and suggested this was another good example of how artificial demarcations can be misleading. "There is nothing but the blood of old roses running through their veins," she said. "I can assure you they look and smell and carry themselves as old roses should."

Still, Eleonora is never quite sure who the parents are. "We know they inherit their type—whether they are climbers or ramblers or shrubs—from their mother," she explained. "Their color, on the other hand, will likely come from the father. Those are useful clues. But other traits, such as the number of petals or the particular fragrance, can come from either parent. So I have an idea who the father and mother might be, but it is never more than an educated guess, and there always remains a considerable uncertainty."

Eleonora takes special delight in the exuberant coupling that occurs in her garden. Every time Valentino alerts her to the birth of a new rose she lets out a cry of excitement. But I've noticed she has only a limited interest in the genealogy of these roses. The mystery that surrounds them suits her romantic temperament. "I hear Japanese scientists have developed a DNA test," she said to me once. "Well, I'm not going to run a test on my roses. I know their parents live in this garden, and that is enough for me."

We were not far from the rose she had named after my ancestor Lucia, so I suggested we go check to see how it was doing. I was surprised to see how much it had grown in a year: it had wrapped itself around a sturdy chestnut pole to reach the top of the pergola, where the sun that morning was shining bright and warm. At the time of the christening the year before, there had been only a couple of blossoms. Now there were dozens of creamy white roses spreading their sweet scent all around us. In light of my personal interest, I asked Eleonora if she had at least a suspicion as to which two roses might have coupled to produce it. She would only say that the dulcet, vaguely exotic fragrance suggested a musk rose, while the vigor of the plant brought to mind a climbing *multiflora*. She seemed disengaged as she spoke, and I wondered if her reticence was related less to the uncertainty of the parentage and more to her unwillingness to pry too deeply in the private affairs of her roses.

The mechanism behind these natural hybrids is simple enough. Drawn by the smell of nectar, a bee lands on one of Eleonora's roses and avidly sucks the sugary substance. In the process, its little legs slip in and out of pollen sacs and get messy with grains containing male sperm. The same bee then wanders over to another rose, and while it loads up on more nectar, the pollen grains from the previous one, still stuck on its legs, are intercepted by the stigma, the female organ of the receiving rose. The sperm travel down to the ovary, where one of them fertilizes an ovule that will in turn produce one of the seeds lodged in the rose hip. In the late fall the hip falls to the ground and eventually cracks open. A seed drops out, germinates, and brings to life a new hybrid.

Any number of insects can pollinate. Butterflies can do the job, even hummingbirds. But in Eleonora's garden, bees do most of the work. This is surprising, because they must travel several miles every day to get back to their hive. The waves of electricity that occasionally sweep through the garden from the nearby railroad keep the queen bee away; but unlike their queen, worker bees don't seem to mind the electricity. So every day in the spring, they fly over to Eleonora's, fill up, and fly back across the countryside. In mid-May, at the height of the blooming season, the garden is abuzz with bloated bees flying in and out like tiny cargo planes.

Bees have a predilection for so-called wild roses, which are for the most part simple flowers with only five open petals and tall stamens and pistils. The bees land easily, move about untrammeled, load up on nectar, and take off. A similar operation on a cabbage rose and other varieties thick with petals would lead to snafus of all kinds.

The term "wild roses" applies to species, and their

natural mutations and forms, which have been growing in different parts of the Northern Hemisphere
since long before man began to cultivate roses. (No
rose species has been known to grow spontaneously in
the Southern Hemisphere.) Some of the better-known
ones are, from Europe, *R. canina, R. eglanteria, R. gallica, R. pimpinellifolia,* and *R. villosa;* from North America, *R. carolina* and *R. virginiana;* from Asia, *R. banksiae,
R. bracteata, R. chinensis, R. multiflora,* and *R. wichurana;*
and from the Middle East, *R. x damascena, R. foetida,* and
R. phoenicia.

These roses have very good genes. They are strong
and bug-resistant. They self-prune and survive in the
harshest climates, from the bitter winters of the Kam-
chatka in Russia to the torrid heat of North Africa.
Eleonora has a very large collection of them: 174 different wild roses at last count. And she believes the
sheer abundance of them in her garden helps explain
the intense pollinating activity. "At least one parent of
each of my hybrids is usually a wild rose."

Eleonora has a sharp, animal-like sense of what goes
on in her garden. Over the years, she has observed how
the hawfinches that have come to nest in the hornbeam
groves play an important role as well. Hawfinches are
not known for their singing, which is really more like a
chirpy mumble. They are bulky little birds, six to eight

inches long, with powerful chests and short tails. Their coat is gray-brown, turning to orange over the head; they wear a black, masklike eye stripe and bib. But their most striking feature is their bill, as hard and compact as an anvil. They smash cherry stones with it; that's how hard it is. So rose hips, even the hardest ones, are easy game. "The hawfinches crack them open, eat the seeds, digest them, and then leave droppings in different parts of the garden," Eleonora told me.

The image of hawfinches flying around the garden planting new roses was compelling, but I wondered if it was supported by science.

When the first of these natural hybrids bloomed in her garden in the late 1990s, Eleonora named it after her husband, Valentino. It turned into a robust climber that now grows on a trellis in a cozy clearing by the house. It has perfect semi-double roses that are creamy white with a hint of yellow toward the center. Oddly, though, they smell of pepper. "My husband was not very happy," Eleonora said to me, taking one of the roses in her hands to smell the peculiar fragrance. "It tickles his nose."

Natural hybrids do not necessarily produce roses

that are to our liking—they may have a disagreeable fragrance or droopy, misshapen petals (though I personally found the peppery fragrance of the rose named after Valentino to be exotic and very enticing). But by and large, the several dozen hybrids I saw in Eleonora's garden were roses of considerable beauty, with lovely, natural colors and delicate fragrances. It was hard to imagine how the great nineteenth-century nurserymen of Lyon could have done a better job than the one nature had done in her garden.

Although Eleonora treats all her natural hybrids with loving attention, when pushed, she will admit to having a favorite. It is a rambling Wichurana with perfectly shaped, semi-double pink-white roses that are intensely fragrant. She named it after her mother, Angiolina. Now fifteen years old, it covers the pergola leading from the back of the house to the garden.

When Eleonora was a little girl she used to follow her mother around their small country garden, up the road from where her house is now, while her father, Bernardo, the town cooper, was at work making barrels for the local wineries. Much of what she knows about flowers and gardening she learned from Angiolina: "She used to grow asters, zinnias, calendulas, peonies, and roses around our old vegetable plot. In the spring the house was full of fresh cuttings from the garden. But on the day of my birthday she would always get up early and go out in the fields and later wake me up with an armful of wildflowers."

Rosa Angiolina is such a beautiful rose—well poised and vigorous and naturally elegant—that it compares

Angiolina

well with the classic hybrids created in the last two hundred years. As I lingered by the pergola on that lovely spring day, I confess that I became so enraptured by the sheer loveliness of the rose that I wondered whether some mysterious form of intelligence might not be behind such a heavenly treasure.

Initially I had assumed that the natural hybrids in Eleonora's garden were the result of random pollination. I pictured the bees buzzing from one flower to another, feasting to their hearts' content, with no particular plan except to follow the whim of the moment. I did not believe that roses had "secret entanglements"—an irritating expression sometimes used by rose experts—that produced spectacular hybrids. Roses such as the one Eleonora had named after Lucia were the accidental products of a bee's wanderings during a day's work.

Or so I thought.

Not long after my second visit to Artegna, I happened to be in Florence on a writing assignment and decided to drive out to see Stefano Mancuso at his lab in Sesto Fiorentino to see what he had to say about the proliferation of hybrids in Eleonora's garden. To my surprise, he immediately took issue with the notion of random pollination. If natural hybridization were a random process, he explained, the results would follow the law of averages and be reflected in a typical bell curve. "We would have a tiny number of beautiful roses with wonderful scents and an equally tiny number of hideous roses with terrible smells. But the vast majority would be rather plain-looking roses with bland fragrances. From what you tell me, this is not the case."

I confirmed that the new hybrids were on the whole

striking, healthy, and fragrant, and that some, such as the Rosa Angiolina, had turned out to be exceptional cultivars.

"The roses themselves could be stage-managing the breeding process by encouraging and facilitating bees to pollinate specific flowers," he said matter-of-factly.

I looked at him with incredulity.

"This is not surprising," he added, smiling. "It is how natural selection works. Animals enact strategies in order to find the right partner. Why shouldn't plants do the same? Selecting a partner is a crucial step in the evolution of a species."

Mancuso cautioned against my thinking about natural selection in human terms. "A rose is looking to survive and to strengthen in its environment, not to please our eyes or excite our nostrils. So what you are likely to get are roses with strong personalities and distinct features rather than roses that might be beautiful according to the fashion of the moment."

I asked Mancuso if Eleonora's simple notion about the hawfinches scattering seeds in the garden made any sense at all.

"Of course it does," he said. "The hip containing the seeds is either clipped off at the time of pruning in early spring or else it falls to the ground, usually near the mother. But in the mother's shadow, the seed has fewer chances of germinating and growing into a robust seedling. Instead, I can imagine a situation in which the mother rose uses its bright colors to attract the hawfinch in the hope that it will crack open the hip, eat the seeds, digest them, and deposit them in another part of the garden where the seedling will have a better chance of making it. Of course, the seed may be dropped in a spot that is even less conducive to growth, but the overall odds of survival improve."

"You speak as if roses were intelligent creatures," I said.

"Because I think they are," Mancuso retorted.

Charles Darwin was the first modern scientist to contemplate the notion held by ancient Greeks that plants are intelligent organisms—Aristotle even thought they had feelings. Toward the end of his life, Darwin became fascinated by the ways plants respond to external stimuli, using and exchanging information to adapt and survive in different environments. In 1880, twenty-one years after the publication of *On the Origin of Species*, he wrote a book called *The Power of Movement in*

Plants, in which he drew attention to the role played by the apices of roots and radicles in the transmission of data in and between plants.

Darwin died two years later, and for a long time no one followed the trail he had opened up. The field was left to New Age and science fiction writers. Even today, most people think of plant intelligence as a paranormal phenomenon. In 1986 the tabloids had a field day when Prince Charles confessed he talked to plants in order to help them grow and stay healthy.

In the mid-1990s, Mancuso and his colleagues finally picked up where Darwin had left off and started looking for scientific evidence of his early insights into plant behavior. They found that plants are endowed with neuronal molecules located in the apices of roots and radicles, as Darwin had imagined. A plant's vascular tissue serves as a highway for rapid signal transmission between the root apices and the organs aboveground. In turn, this constant flow of information allows the plant to acquire and process data, to develop learning abilities, and to form memory. According to Mancuso, the information traffic is directed by an underground "brain" that is structured like a web, with each apex of the root system acting as a signal post.

Since plants are fixed in the ground, they must manage their immediate environment in order to survive. How they gather, process, use, and transmit information to draw certain insects to them when they need them and to repel others when they are threatened; how they attract light; how they ensure a proper supply of moisture and nutrients—it is all a matter of life and death. "Plants are more sensitive to their surroundings than animals," Mancuso told me. "Including humans."

In his view, Eleonora's great achievement is to have created an environment where her roses feel comfortable enough to relinquish their reticence and give in to a real yearning to multiply and diversify. "If one loves plants the way she does, if one holds them and talks to them and makes them feel they are welcome, they will perceive human warmth."

He paused before adding, "I don't think I would be using these exact words in a conversation with my colleagues."

At first Eleonora named the new hybrids after close friends and members of her family. But the roses kept coming out of the ground every spring, and soon she ran out of family and friends to name them after. So she started naming them after Friulan women who had inspired her.

One day I noticed a solitary climber stretching out against the metal fence that separated the garden from the railroad tracks. The large, semi-double roses were a delicate white that turned to lilac toward the center. Valentino had spotted this rose several years earlier, in a small clearing on the other side of the garden, and Eleonora later had him move it to its current location. I thought it was an unusual place to plant a rose—out of the way and in full view of the tracks—but it seemed happy to be where it was and now covered a good portion of the fence.

Eleonora had named the rose after Pierina di Brazzà-Savorgnan Cergneu, a schoolteacher who had lived nearby. Pierina was something of a legend in the region. She was born in 1846 in Gorizia, a small city that is now on the border with Slovenia but was then part of the Austro-Hungarian Empire. Her father belonged to an impoverished branch of the Savorgnan, an old Friulan family. Pierina grew up on a farm outside Nimis, a town six miles down the road from Artegna. She married a civil engineer, and they had several children. In the 1890s her husband was sent to Irkutsk, in central Siberia, to oversee the building of the Trans-Siberian Railroad. In those years, several thousand Friulani migrated to Siberia to work on the Trans-Siberian line, which was one of the most ambitious engineering projects of its time. They were hard workers, especially valued for their skills as masons, stonecutters, and stone dressers.

Pierina was already in her fifties when she followed her husband to Siberia. She settled in Irkutsk, taught Latin and French at the local high school, and took a special interest in the welfare of the Friulani workers. She was known as "Mother of the Italian Workers." A highly educated woman, she drafted reports on working conditions in Siberia for international labor organizations and wrote articles on Russian affairs for Italian and German newspapers.

When World War I broke out, her husband was in Italy. She was cut off from Friuli and stayed on in Irkutsk, surviving the horrors of the Revolution of 1917 and the even greater horrors of the Russian Civil War, when Irkutsk became the scene of fierce battles between the Red Army and the White Russians. The city was destroyed, thousands of civilians were killed, and women were raped and mutilated. Pierina lost all her possessions when her house was doused with petrol and set on fire. Yet she made it through. At the age of seventy-four, in the dead of winter, she left the smoldering city behind her and started the long journey home, walking along the broken railway tracks of the Trans-Siberian all the way to Vladivostok, at the end of the Russian Empire.

Pierina left an account of her extraordinary journey, a copy of which is in the town library in Nimis. It is a gripping tale of endurance in which she describes the hardships of extreme temperatures and the frequent threat of famished wolves and dangerous brigands. But there are also moments of touching lyricism recounted by this tiny human speck inching her way forward in the silent, never-ending Siberian landscape: "The days went by, always the same, and the weeks and the months. The heavy furs we had to wear slowed us down, and we managed only short distances, though sometimes a sled would come swishing out of nowhere and give us a lift. There was nothing to see, only snow, snow, snow. A shining white mantle stretched into infinite nothing-ness, broken here and there in the distance by a grove of firs. White Siberian hares shooting across our path like big fluffy snowballs caused the only movement in that otherwise absolute stillness."

In the spring, Pierina reached Vladisvostok, where she was able to board a ship carrying Italian prisoners of war back to Trieste. She eventually made it back to

Nimis and resumed teaching in the local school. She died at the age of ninety.

Inspired by Pierina's life, Eleonora named the new rose after her. The usual christening ceremony was held in the garden—only this time there was quite a little crowd in attendance, with local officials, including the mayor of Artegna, pressing to have their picture taken holding the stem with the first blossom.

When the guests were gone, Eleonora asked Valentino to plant the little rose over by the fence near the railroad tracks.

"It's not the Trans-Siberian," she told me, "but I thought it would be a nice way to remember her."

This lovely rose, and all the other natural hybrids that have come to life under Eleonora's watchful eye, will only ever grow in her garden. Few people will have the opportunity to see them. True, every spring busloads of rose lovers come to Artegna, and not just from within Friuli but from neighboring Austria and Slovenia. But these are relatively small numbers compared to the millions all over the world who would be happy to cultivate them in their rose gardens.

Eleonora, however, is not in business. To sell her roses, she would have to register them with the International Cultivar Registration Authority, which is run by the American Rose Society, and then purchase commercial rights. Registration is free, but commercial rights, which would give her the exclusive right to produce and sell her roses, can be expensive—up to several hundred dollars a year per cultivar. That is more than she and Valentino can afford. But money is not all. "I am not a trader at heart," she confessed, "and I can't imagine selling these roses."

The one exception for which she occasionally contemplates the idea of purchasing commercial rights is Rosa Angiolina. "It is really such a beautiful rose. Making it available to others would be a nice way of honoring my mother."

I teased Eleonora, reminding her that Empress Josephine, whom she admired, was very generous with her roses. "If you don't want to sell them, why don't you give cuttings away? The roses would propagate and have a greater chance of surviving."

Eleonora was silent for a while. Then she said, "I think I like the idea that people have to come here to see them."

CHAPTER SEVEN

Orphan Roses

few years ago Eleonora ran out of space for her roses. Fortunately, she was able to purchase an extra half acre of land from her neighbor, down at the end of the garden. The new plot had not been worked for over thirty years. Valentino cleared the brush and brambles, leaving only the trees standing—a large elm, a willow, an ash, and a walnut. It is now a lovely spot, with a full view of the castle of Artegna, straight up the hill, and the mountains rising behind it.

For all Valentino's hard work, it remains the wildest part of the garden. And it is where Eleonora keeps her *rose ritrovate*, her "rediscovered roses"—long-lost old shrubs she has found in the woods, among ruins, or in old country cemeteries. "I chose to put them there because they are used to living in a rough environment," she once told me.

I have counted 153 different species and varieties of *rose ritrovate*, clustered in three separate patches. Some of them still look rather untamed, compared to the worldly roses that consort in the more refined parts of the garden.

Eleonora calls these old shrubs her "orphan roses"

because she has yet to identify the parents. She can usually tell what class each one belongs to—whether it is a Gallica or an Alba, a Damask, or a Centifolia—but little more. So she keeps them under close observation, in the hope that sooner or later a small detail—the number of prickles or the particular shape of the leaves or the color of the hips in autumn—will reveal enough about a particular rose that she will make the right genealogical connections, determine the group it belongs to, and give it back its name.

So far this has happened only once. A woman from the nearby town of Tarcento brought Eleonora a rose she'd found in an old vegetable patch. Little thin leaves grew around each bud—the typical trait of *R. x centifolia foliacea*, a rose that Josephine had at Malmaison. Redouté included it in his famous rose book, and Eleonora instantly recognized it.

However, the odds are that, for all their splendor and fragrance, these toughened old roses will live on in anonymity. Even in the month of May, when they put on a show of unspeakable beauty, an aching melancholy hangs over this part of the garden.

It is here that Eleonora has planted the Rosa Moceniga that De Rocco brought to her shortly before his death. It grows between two anonymous shrubs. One is a crimson Gallica found near the entrance of a small chapel in an old graveyard in Modena, a city in the Po Valley famous for its balsamic vinegar. The other is a very large and stalwart shrub that produces a gorgeous scarlet rose. "A couple from Artegna traveled to Romania during the summer holidays," Eleonora told me. "They went into the woods looking for mushrooms and found this rosebush, which they smuggled back to me. It is also a Gallica of some kind, a very old rose." She handed me a few petals. "See how sweet they taste. I was told they make rose marmalade with them in Romania."

In the spring, several thousand visitors come through Eleonora's garden to see her roses, but she seldom brings them to the back of the garden. Although she checks on her "orphans" every day to track their development, she keeps them at a certain distance, even from herself. I wouldn't say she is indifferent to them, but she doesn't show the same degree of intimacy that she does with the roses in other parts of the garden. I asked her about this, and she said she didn't really think of them as her own. "I see myself as a custodian; I look after them as best I can, but I don't feel they belong to me."

Near the entrance of her "orphanage," where the garden narrows like a funnel, Eleonora has planted an impressive purple Gallica that stands there like a sentinel. It is called 'Dis-Moi Qui Je Suis'—"Tell Me Who I Am." Its wonderful name has made it the symbol of unidentified old roses. Several nurseries now sell it, although the mystery persists: What is the real name of this rose? Where does it originally come from?

I got in touch with Eléonore Cruse, the woman who sold Eleonora the rose, because I was curious to know if she had any idea who had thought of calling it 'Dis-Moi Qui Je Suis'. "Why, it was me!" Madame Cruse shot back cheerfully over the phone. She had found the rose on the property of a farmer two miles away from her nursery of old roses in the village of Berty, in the Rhône-Alpes. "It is probably a late-nineteenth-century cross between a Gallica and a Chinese rose," she added.

Dis-Moi Qui Je Suis

"I gave it a *nom d'attente,* a temporary name, in the hope that one day someone will discover its real one."

*n*ow that old roses are back in fashion it is easy to forget that they came very close to extinction. When targeted hybridization spread at the start of the twentieth century, hordes of brightly colored, reflowering roses invaded the market. Demand for old roses plummeted. Nurseries dropped them from their catalogs and stopped breeding them altogether. The loss was massive and very swift. If some of them survived at all, it was thanks to a handful of dedicated rose lovers.

Graham Stuart Thomas, the great English garden designer and rose expert, was the principal force behind the revival of old rose shrubs that got under way in the 1970s. He started out in the late 1930s as an apprentice nurseryman at the Botanic Garden at Cambridge University. At the time, he had no particular interest in old roses, and was in fact "almost repelled" by the mauve-pinks and purples of those few varieties he was able to see during his early garden tours in England and Ireland. The world of old roses was vanishing fast, but few people seemed to care, and Thomas was not among them.

In those days the last great remaining private collection of old roses belonged to Edward Bunyard, a gardener of taste and a man of culture. He was, among other things, Britain's premier pomologist, or apple expert. Less known is the role he played during the two wars in bringing together increasingly rare species and varieties of old roses. Bunyard killed himself in 1939, and his rose collection was put up for sale. It seemed like the death knell of a disappearing world.

Before the sale went through, young Graham Thomas was sent out to take a look at the collection. This time, however, he was entranced by what he later described as "the treasure stored by this enlightened man." A lifelong passion was ignited. It was not easy to travel around England during the war years, but Thomas nevertheless managed to assemble his own small collection of old rose shrubs.

His efforts came to the attention of the formidable Constance Spry, a tastemaker and lifestyle guru of English society in the 1940s and '50s. The daughter of a railway clerk, Mrs. Spry had started out as a social worker in Hackney before opening a florist shop and eventually transforming herself into the Martha Stewart of the pillbox-hat era. But in her private life, she devoted herself to the cultivation of old roses. She was very generous with her knowledge and helped Thomas when he was starting out. When the time came to disband her collection, Mrs. Spry turned to her young friend to propagate her roses—a symbolic passing of the torch and a considerable addition to Thomas's own collection. She died in 1960. The following year, Thomas collaborated with the rose breeder David Austin to create the famous 'Constance Spry', the first of the so-called English roses—a climber with clear pink blooms obtained from a Gallica and a Floribunda, which has become a very popular rose.

After the war, when petrol was again available, Thomas cast a wider net, hunting for old roses as far north as Yorkshire. He benefited from the encouragement of old rose lovers of an earlier generation, such as Vita Sackville-West at Sissinghurst and Sacheverell Sitwell at Weston Hall. By 1948 he had assembled what was arguably the greatest collection of old roses—it included shrubs from France, Germany, and the United States. Now part of the National Trust, the collection is happily ensconced in an old walled garden at Mottisfont Abbey, in Hampshire, which Thomas designed.

The Old Shrub Roses, Thomas's first book, has been a classic ever since it was published in 1955. It has inspired several generations of gardeners not only to plant and propagate old roses but to go out of their way to find lost species and varieties that might still survive in the countryside, untended and forgotten.

The Italian edition of *The Old Shrub Roses* was published in the 1970s under the editorial supervision of Ippolito Pizzetti, who was then Italy's best-known botanist. "It was the first book on roses I ever bought," Eleonora told me. "There were hardly any books available here in Artegna. I had a bookstore from Turin send it to me, and I remember the excitement when the postman arrived at the house. I never had the opportunity to meet Thomas, but his book had such an impact on me that I still consider him my spiritual guide."

Eleonora became obsessed with the task of saving forgotten old roses that were growing in the wild in her native Friuli. Thomas's hunting grounds were, for the most part, the grand old gardens of England. Eleonora, on the other hand, had Valentino drive her around the countryside and up into the mountains behind Artegna. She met with countless Friulani who still had old roses growing in their vegetable gardens and orchards, and who happily gave her cuttings. Within a short time, she had collected dozens of nameless shrubs. Then De Rocco started parking his own rediscovered roses with her. Other friends and neighbors appeared on her doorstep. Word spread, and soon even strangers were coming by the house bearing cuttings in small pots or plastic bags. They came from Gemona, Tricesimo, Tarcento, Nimis, and other nearby Friulan towns. But as Eleonora's reputation grew, people started driving over from other regions and even from across the border with Austria and Slovenia.

Thomas's rediscovered roses were more easily identifiable because they came mostly from old English gardens. Eleonora, on the other hand, was gathering old roses that no one seemed to know. To each of these old shrubs, she gave a temporary name—usually the name of the person who'd brought her the plant or else the name of the place where it was found.

The first "orphan" Eleonora took in was a globular pink rose she inherited from her mother, who had in turn inherited it from *her* mother. It is a stalwart shrub, and the roses are packed with petals. The leaves and stems are coated with sticky fuzz.

Eleonora thinks it is probably a cross between an *R. x centifolia* and an *R. x centifolia* var. *muscosa*. She remembers seeing it for the first time in the vegetable garden her grandmother kept in Jouf, a small hamlet up in the mountains behind Artegna. (*Jouf* means "wolf" in Friulan.) When she was a little girl, during the war, her mother used to take her and her two sisters to visit their grandmother once a week. It was a two-hour walk up a steep path. In the winter, it was cold and dark and the little hamlet was bleak. But in the spring and the summer, the girls enjoyed the trek. They drank from the stream, ate plums in the orchards along the way, and picked *fuees di garoful,* the petals of wild roses, and *puntes di baracs,* the crunchy, sweet-tasting buds on blackberry bushes. The climb always turned into a feast.

The grandmother's vegetable patch was on a small family plot one reached before the hamlet. The girls would make the last turn along the pathway to Jouf, and there it was, standing pretty and proud: the beloved *garoful dal muscli*, which in the Friulan language means the "mossy rose."

"I am not sure how the rose came into the family," Eleonora told me as we drove up to Jouf one day. "My grandmother's family was better off than my grandfather's, and I suspect she brought it with her when she married him in 1890. But it is also possible an old aunt of mine brought a cutting from the castle that belonged to the counts of Gemona, where she had gone to work as a cleaning lady when my father's side of the family fell on hard times."

The old path was now a road, and it took us no more

than fifteen minutes to drive from Artegna up to Jouf. There were only a few old houses left, a fountain, and a washing trough. Eleonora's grandmother's house was still standing, but the old family vegetable garden no longer existed; the woodland had taken over.

On the way home, about halfway down the winding road to Artegna, Eleonora asked Valentino to stop the car. "We used to leave Jouf at dusk," she said, "so that by the time we reached this bend in the path it was quite dark. My mother told us the *partigiani* shot a young German soldier here and left him by the side of the path to die. Every time we passed by this spot I quickened my pace in fear."

The Germans occupied Artegna in 1943, after the fall of Mussolini. But the soldiers never ventured up in the mountains alone because they would have been easy prey for the *partigiani,* the resistance fighters who took up arms against the Nazis. I asked Eleonora why a German soldier would have wandered up here. "The young man had fallen in love with a girl who lived there," she said, pointing to a farmhouse near the road. "Every day, he came up to see her even though he knew he was risking his life. Finally the *partigiani* ambushed him, but they didn't kill him, and he lay there in agony for three days. His cries kept everyone awake at the farmhouse, but no one dared to bring him in for fear of being killed.

The soldier finally died of his wounds. When the Germans came to fetch the body, they threatened to torch the farmhouse. In the end they were persuaded that the *partigiani* were behind the killing."

After the war someone planted a cross where the soldier had died. There were always fresh flowers near it. Everyone assumed this was the doing of the young woman with whom the German had fallen in love. But years went by, the woman became old and died, and still there were flowers by the cross. In the village it was said that the family was so filled with remorse for not coming out to save the German that the younger generations continued to bring flowers.

We got out of the car and walked over to the rusty old iron cross by the road. Seventy years had passed since the soldier was killed. There were blue and yellow plastic flowers in a pot by the grave. "I guess it's late in the season," Eleonora said. "The flowers are usually fresh."

Although the grandmother's old vegetable garden up at Jouf no longer exists, the pink rose has survived. "When my mother married my father," Eleonora explained to me, "she brought it with her to Artegna as part of her trousseau. She planted it in our vegetable garden, up the road from the house we lived in. In May, when the rose bloomed, she would wake us up and say, 'Come and see the *garoful dal muscli*!' My sisters and I would get out of bed in a hurry, get dressed, and head up the hill, running and skipping to my mother's vegetable patch. She made us hold the rose and rub the sticky moss on our fingers and smell the wonderful fragrance. It wasn't spiced or fruity, just *profumo di rose,* the typical sweet scent of a rose. It flowered once a year."

She smiled thinking of those happy scenes of her childhood. "Our visits to the *garoful dal muscli* were a joy."

After the flower had bloomed, Eleonora's mother would gather the petals before they fell to the ground, bring them down to the house, and spread them in the linen closet. Eleonora still remembers the *profumo di rose* she smelled every time she went to fetch sheets for the beds. "When I married Valentino my mother gave me the *garoful dal muscli* as part of my own trousseau. I suppose that, in her mind, the rose was meant to go with the linen. It's been with me ever since, although I am ashamed to say that I don't much use it in the linen closet. After all these years I still don't know what its proper name is. My sisters and I have always called it *la rosa della Mamma*"—"Mama's rose."

Eleonora has a daughter, Ornella, but she did not give her a *garoful dal muscli* when she married. "She lives with her family in an apartment in the city," she explained. "Perhaps my son, Dino, will marry. He is forty-nine, but one must never lose hope." For the time being it looks like a family tradition will come to an end. But the shrub still grows among the other orphan roses, hardy and proud like an old veteran. Every time I visit Eleonora, I go see how it is doing. I take one of the big roses in my hand and feel the sticky fuzz on my fingers and lean down to smell the familiar *profumo di rose*.

Among the orphans is another hardy shrub, covered with beautiful white roses. Eleonora told me this rose used to grow in great profusion in the gardens of the nearby Abbey of Rosazzo, an eleventh-century fortress-monastery set among old vineyards that stretch out to the beginning hills of Slovenia. It is a very old rose—one recognizes it in the sixteenth-century frescoes that adorn the presbytery of the church—and it came to symbolize the abbey. The monks simply called it *la Rosa di Rosazzo,* but it was never clear what kind of rose it was or where it came from. Then one day all the roses died.

The story of how the cultivar survived is one Eleonora loves to tell.

In 1915, the year Italy entered World War I, the abbey was turned into a military hospital. Eastern Friuli was a major battleground. The front line separating Italian and Austro-Hungarian soldiers was never far from Rosazzo. In May 1917, five months before the Austrian troops broke through the lines and invaded Friuli, a young corporal was brought in on a stretcher. His name was Giovanni Cobai and his legs had been badly hit by an enemy grenade near Gorizia. His brother Luigi came to visit, and he brought with him a young friend, Beniamino Pascolo. Before going up to see Giovanni, the two stopped in the abbey's garden, which was just then in full bloom, to gather a bouquet of the lovely white roses of Rosazzo.

After the war, Pascolo, like many young Friulans without a job, left Italy, migrating to Lorraine, in France, to work in the mines. Before leaving, knowing that he might never come back to his beloved Friuli, he went back to the Abbey of Rosazzo—he remembered the roses that grew in that garden and he wished to take a cutting with him to France.

A few years later, in 1929, a devastating winter freeze killed all the roses at the abbey—every single one. The fabled *Rosa di Rosazzo* was lost—or so it was thought for about sixty years, until one fine spring day, Beniamino's grandson, Jean-Marc Pascolo, appeared on the abbey's doorstep. He had traveled from France to check on some old family property in Friuli and, having heard so much about the abbey from his grandfather, had come to pay a visit. When Pascolo asked Don Dino Pezzetta, the abbot, if he could see the famous white rose of Rosazzo, he was told about the great freeze of 1929.

"But I have many shrubs of it growing in my garden in France!" Pascolo exclaimed.

The following year, he returned with a splendid specimen of *la Rosa di Rosazzo,* which now grows again at the abbey. On that return visit, Pascolo met Eleonora, and after visiting her garden, he decided it would be prudent to give her a cutting as well.

"Just in case there is another cold spell," she said to me, chuckling.

*E*very time I go to Artegna, I am drawn to the brooding restlessness of the orphan shrubs at the far end of the garden. Over by the three great vegetable plots, where all the fancy roses grow, the atmosphere is livelier and more sophisticated, and I enjoy following Eleonora around as she recounts the story of Madame This and Madame That. But there comes a point when the orphans beckon, and I find myself working my way toward them.

When the weather is nice, I lie down in the shade of the great walnut tree and gaze at these roses. They are the rough kids on the block. Plucked from the wild, they warily guard their secrets; they keep their distance. Unlike the other roses, which are always putting on a show, begging to tell their story, the orphans don't like to chat—and their silence can be unsettling.

Most of these stray roses will remain nameless, their pasts forgotten, their identities erased. But will they one day let down their defenses and speak to one another in the language of roses? Will bees and hawfinches work their magic and help these orphans spread their seeds? Will there be new life in this part of the garden, and new roses?

One afternoon, I was still daydreaming under the great walnut tree when I heard Eleonora calling out to me from the house.

"Monsieur Joyaux is coming! Monsieur Joyaux is coming!"

Our friend Benedetta had been hard at work organizing another two-day rose festival at Cordovado. It now turned out that she had secretly extended an invitation to Monsieur Joyaux, and much to her surprise, he had accepted. He would be traveling by car from France with Madame Joyaux. They asked whether a visit at Alvisopoli to see the Rosa Moceniga might be arranged, as well as a trip to Artegna.

"Imagine!" Eleonora exclaimed after filling me in. "Monsieur Joyaux himself will come here to see my roses!" Although his visit was months away, she was already in a state of agitation. "We must get to work," she said, turning to Valentino. "There is so much to do!"

The unflappable Valentino was duly impressed this time. "Monsieur Joyaux," he mumbled to himself. "I'll be damned."

As we said good-bye, Eleonora asked me if I spoke French, and I said yes.

"Then you will be Monsieur Joyaux's interpreter during his visit."

CHAPTER EIGHT

Eleonora and Valentino

Valentino met Eleonora at a country wedding in 1957, when Friuli was a poor rural region still badly scarred by the war. He was from the nearby town of Gemona, where he worked as a bus driver and mechanic—a strapping eighteen-year-old with a shock of dirty blond hair and an easy smile.

"She was wearing one of those wide skirts that were popular in the fifties," Valentino said. We were having lunch at his favorite trattoria in Artegna, and after a few glasses of Cabernet, he became more talkative than usual. "I remember she had a tight white shirt on."

"Lilac," Eleonora corrected him. "Both the skirt and the shirt were lilac." She was nineteen at the time. "I wouldn't even have looked at him if I had known he was a year younger than me."

Valentino became a familiar sight in Artegna, his big, strong hands at the wheel as he steered the clunky old bus through narrow village streets and up and down the mountain roads behind the town. Eleonora had finished commercial school, and her father, Bernardo, the town cooper, had found her a job as an accountant at the local winery. The family lived in a rustic old house that was later destroyed in the 1976 earthquake. Her room looked out onto the open courtyard, where vats and barrels were stacked against the walls. Beyond it were fields filled with flowers and fruit trees.

Each time Valentino drove his bus through Artegna, he would pass in front of the winery and honk three times, and Eleonora would come out to wave at him. He wooed her for five years, including three years when he was away on military duty. They were married in 1963. Eleonora kept her job at the winery until their son, Dino, was born. A few years later Ornella was born. Valentino stayed on with the bus company, eventually rising to management.

Now well into his seventies, Valentino has taken his retirement but claims he has never worked so hard in his life. He and Eleonora put in long, exhausting days tending the roses and the vegetable plots. Valentino is out of the house at six in the morning wearing battle fatigues—in the winter, when the ground needs more time to soften, he goes out a bit later, wearing a black woolen cap to keep his balding head warm. Eleonora, neatly dressed and with just the right amount of makeup, including her fuschia lipstick, follows shortly afterward and starts giving him orders.

There is no doubt about who is in charge in the garden. "She tells me where to dig," Valentino says. "She tells me when to cut and when to prune. In the garden, I am happy to let her be the boss. Besides, I don't know the first thing about roses. I don't even know what I am planting."

It takes one look at their luxuriant, beautifully kept garden to realize Valentino is playing dumb—of course he knows what he's planting, but he feigns ignorance so he can leave all the serious decision making to his wife. Eleonora is naturally inclined to take the initiative, self-confident to the point of appearing bossy. This division of labor suits their characters. Valentino feels more comfortable taking orders and carrying them out well. "Give me the right coordinates—give me my longitude and my latitude—and I'll get you there," he says.

At noon Eleonora goes back to the house and fixes lunch. Cooking is not really her forte. She prepares practical, easy-to-assemble meals. To save time, she will stand over the stove on rainy days and cook large amounts of stew and vegetables, which she then stores in the freezer. "When I come in from the garden all I have to do is set the table and warm up the food," she says. Valentino walks in at 12:30 sharp, takes the muck off his boots, and sits down at the table. He always goes by the clock; it upsets him when people are not on time and mess up his schedule. His obsession with punctuality is a carryover from his days as a bus driver. But since he allows Eleonora to have her way in the garden, she makes sure his meal is ready on time.

In other ways as well, Valentino is a man of fixed habits. Every day, he has two glasses of the same Cabernet with his lunch, followed by an espresso laced with grappa. Then he is ready to go back into the garden and work until dark. Eleonora leaves the dishes for later. While Valentino puts his lumberjack boots back on, she straightens her clothes, arranges her hair, and puts on more fuchsia lipstick. I asked her why she bothered with the lipstick, since she was just going out to weed and grub in the garden.

"I like to look right when I go back to my roses," she said without missing a beat.

Although Valentino takes pleasure from most of his activities in the garden, he is happiest when he can use his *motosega,* his chain saw. "The moment I put my right foot forward and get in position, I feel in complete control. I know I will get the job done properly. Besides, I have no choice. If I cut the wrong limb—no, the wrong *twig*—she will come after me with a cudgel and give me no peace."

Eleonora grins. "He's afraid to make mistakes. I have to be mindful about what I say or he'll get all bothered and defensive."

They will, occasionally, get on each other's nerves. One day we were out in the garden and Valentino was way up in a tree sawing off old wood. He was lashed to a branch with nothing more than a sling. Eleonora was looking up and shouting orders: "Cut there! . . . And over there!" I could see Valentino was getting annoyed. After a while he yelled back at her, "Get lost! . . . Let me work!" Eleonora turned to me in mock surprise. "He does this all the time: gets all worked up and sends me on my way," she said. "Stay here with him . . . I'll head off to some other part of the garden and find work to do while he calms down. Soon enough he'll start to feel nostalgic and will call out to me."

After a while Valentino climbed down the tree like a flustered old cat. "Sometimes she just won't understand," he said, brushing twigs and bits of bark off his fatigues. "If I lost my concentration for even a second up there I would drop to the ground like a ripe persimmon."

After he had calmed down, he gathered his tools, ready for the next task.

"Where did she go?" he asked. I pointed in the direction she had headed, and he went looking for her. After a while I heard him cry out in Friulan, *"Eleonora! La se tu lade a finile!"*—"Eleonora! Where the hell have you gone?"

They cannot afford to bear a grudge for very long. With no outside help in the garden, time is always short. The daily work can be exhausting, but they can't fall behind. So, despite the occasional dustup, they run a tight, efficient two-person team. "Every day, I feel we are climbing a steep mountain," she says. "Up and up and up. There is no time to stop and catch our breath. Then, suddenly, in the second part of May, we finally reach the top of the mountain, as it were, and the garden all around us explodes. It doesn't last very long— two weeks at the most. Then we slowly come down the mountain and gather our forces for another long climb the following year. This is our life. Rushing, rushing, rushing, all year round to get the garden ready for when the roses bloom. I am not interested in having a perfect garden. But I want my roses to feel that everything is right. Often I will wake up in the middle of the night with a start, worried that we are lagging behind. I shake Valentino and tell him I can't do it anymore. I tell him I want to get rid of the garden and sell the house. Then I think no one will buy the house, and we'll get stuck with the garden. I get very agitated, so he gets out of bed, puts his clothes on, and goes out in the garden in the dark, because he knows the only way I will calm down is if he's out there working."

In the evening, after dinner, Valentino settles into his armchair by the woodstove and flicks through specialty catalogs advertising lawn mowers, grass cutters and trimmers, brush cutters, chain saws, and other heavy-duty gardening gear. Eleonora clears the table, then pulls out her books and folders and gets down to work. In neat, large capital letters she writes down information she has collected that day in the garden, or else she copies out something she has read in a book. She fills out slips of paper and places them in her neatly arranged folders. She has filled hundreds of folders over the last twenty years. Two bedrooms have been converted into storage rooms where boxes full of her notes and clippings are piled high.

Valentino has offered to provide her some very good software that would save her a lot of time and ensure that all the information in her head and in her paper files is stored on a hard disk as well. But Eleonora continues to prefer her pencil to a computer. "She's a *testa dura*" (a hardheaded woman), Valentino mutters by the fire as he watches his wife hunched over the dinner table like a schoolgirl going over her homework.

*F*rom mid-May to early July, when the garden is in full bloom, rose lovers flock to Artegna. The numbers increase every year. Last time I asked, Eleonora told me that twenty-five hundred visitors had come by to see the garden, not just from Friuli but from Austria, Slovenia, and even Germany as well. The spontaneous hybrids are a big draw. Some rose collectors come back year after year to see the newborns.

Despite Eleonora's growing notoriety, the garden is constantly under threat by unscrupulous local politicians and greedy developers who want to take away her land. Only a few years ago the town government informed her and Valentino that the plot they had just bought to place the orphan roses and a good portion of the old garden were going to be expropriated in order to make way for a large *centro polifunzionale*, a center for arts, entertainment, and social activities.

"Valentino and I were in a state of shock," Eleonora recalls. "Half the garden would have been destroyed." They recovered and went to work. In only a few days they were able to collect more than fifteen hundred signatures in Artegna and the surrounding countryside. That's a lot of signatures in such a small town. The local newspaper covered the protest movement, and the mayor suddenly felt the heat. In the end, the municipal government went ahead with a reduced version of the project and did not expropriate the land.

The *centro polifunzionale* has been under construction for several years now, in fits and starts. Local funds have dried up, the economy is mired in deep recession, and it looks like the tract of land next to Eleonora and Valentino's rose garden will become a permanent eyesore. Even if it is completed one day, it is hard to imagine what use a small town such as Artegna could ever have for such a sprawling center for social activity.

Although Eleonora and Valentino were able to neutralize the threat to their land on that particular occasion, the experience was sobering. She keeps the newspaper clippings about their battle in a folder, and regularly pulls them out to remind herself of how precarious the situation still is.

I often wonder what will happen to the garden once she and Valentino are no longer able to take care of it. For how many more years will he lug his heavy equipment around, climb trees, dig ditches, and plant roses and vegetables? How much longer will she spend the whole day, in the heat and the cold, trudging from one side of the property to the other to check on her roses? They will soon need outside help. But even if they came to accept the idea of someone younger coming in to assist them with the heavier tasks, they probably would not be able to pay him or her out of Valentino's pension.

And suppose the weather took a nasty turn and seriously damaged the garden. Where would they find the resources to get it back into shape?

"I am no longer a spring chicken," Eleonora concedes. "And Valentino won't be able to climb trees for much longer." But every time I ask her if they have made plans for the future, she becomes evasive and invariably brings up a poignant story Lucia mentions in her Paris diary about André Du Pont, the collector who provided Empress Josephine with many of her roses.

Originally from the Rhine region, Du Pont moved to Paris in the late 1770s and settled in the nurserymen's quarter near the Jardin du Luxembourg, quickly establishing his reputation as an expert on roses. After finding employment with the postal service, he continued to build his collection, importing rare roses from abroad, breeding new varieties, buying and selling high-quality cultivars. Empress Josephine took him under her wing and became his principal customer. In 1808 alone, she bought fifteen hundred rosebushes from Du Pont. Grateful for her patronage, he created *R. alba carnea Josephina,* a pale white rose that I believe is now extinct.

Du Pont's collection was by far the largest in France. Although his sales catalog for 1809 lists only 100 species and varieties, he had 537 in his garden on rue de

la Fontaine-au-Roi, in the Faubourg-du-Temple. Lucia
went to see him several times at Josephine's urging. He
confided in her, telling her how much he still missed his
wife, Louise, who had died twelve years earlier, leaving him utterly bereft. One day he brought Lucia to a
secluded spot in the garden where he had buried his
wife's heart; clipped ivy grew over the burial ground in
the shape of a heart. Du Pont told Lucia he wanted his
own heart buried next to his wife's.

It was a difficult time for him. He had reached his
retirement the year before, in 1813, after thirty-five
years of employment in the postal service, and he could
no longer afford the rent at rue de la Fontaine-au-Roi
on his small pension. Without land, he would have to get
rid of his collection. In fact, he had already announced,
to the consternation of his customers, that he had been
forced to quit his business. At least one wealthy for-
eigner offered to purchase his entire collection, provided Du Pont came along, too, but Du Pont declined.
He wished to spend his old age in Paris.

However, by the time Lucia paid Du Pont her last
visit before returning to Italy, a solution had been
found. Du Pont had long eyed a spot in his beloved
Jardin du Luxembourg as the perfect location for his
roses: it was a terraced garden in front of the sixteenth-

century *hôtel particulier* known as the Petit Luxembourg. He had approached the government to offer his
entire collection of roses in exchange for an additional
pension. Count de Sémonville, a high-ranking member
of the House of Peers, at the Palais du Luxembourg,
interceded in his favor, and a deal was struck. The roses
were moved to the Jardin du Luxembourg; in return,
Du Pont was to receive 600 francs a year, in quarterly
installments, enough for him to rent a small apartment
on rue de la Vieille Estrapade.

Later that spring Napoleon's army was defeated, the
allies occupied Paris, and the empire collapsed. Lucia
returned to Italy and never saw Du Pont again. It was
Monsieur Joyaux who pieced together the rest of the
story after finding several of Du Pont's letters in the
Archives de Paris.

After the fall of Napoleon, the Bourbon monarchy
was restored, but the state bureaucracy fell into disar-
ray. When Du Pont went to collect the quarterly install-
ment of his pension on April 1, 1817, a clerk told him it
had been *supprimée*—"canceled." Du Pont wrote three
times to Count Sémonville, but received no reply. In
desperation, he wrote directly to the chief of staff of the
Maison Royale, illustrating his plight and adding that he
was already falling behind on his rent payments. But his

pension was not restored, and Du Pont died in poverty later that year.

The sad ending of Monsieur Du Pont's life had left a deep impression on Eleonora. "Poor man, he was left without his pension *or* his roses," she says every time. "I hope someone remembered to bury his heart next to that of his wife, Louise."

All collectors eventually face the question of what will happen to their roses once they are gone. Some entrust their rare cultivars to other collectors; others establish foundations to ensure that their roses survive, or else bequeath their collection to some botanical garden. Others, still, work for a more permanent solution. Graham Thomas, for one, designed a home for his old roses at Mottisfont Abbey before placing them in care of the National Trust. Important collections often belong to large estates, so they are more likely to survive—one thinks of Sissinghurst or Castle Howard. But many other collections, even great ones, have been entirely lost.

Josephine's garden at Malmaison, for example, went to seed within a very short time—in fact, the reason we know as much about her roses as we do is because Redouté painted them. Eleonora once read to me some lines by Georgette Ducrest, a nineteenth-century memoirist who knew Josephine in her youth and returned to Malmaison a few years after the empress's death: "I hardly recognized the park. The rare shrubs she had planted everywhere had been pulled out and sold. Where the rhododendron had once lined the alleyway, there was nothing but a gaping hole filled with weeds; and tall lucern grass grew in place of those pretty flowerbeds. Destruction was never more swift and complete."

The thought of those gaping holes at Malmaison still haunts Eleonora. "I wouldn't want that for my roses," she says. But as far as I know she has no plans to sell her collection or disperse her cultivars so as to ensure they will survive—not even the homegrown hybrids that exist only in her garden. In fact, she seems inclined to do nothing at all. "I have loved my roses," she says. "They have given me so much joy. They will perhaps return to wilderness when I am gone. I am not worried."

Valentino likes to tease her. "When we're gone," he says, "they will come here with a *tarup*." *Tarup* is Friulan for a heavy brush cutter. "I tell you, they will come here with a *tarup* and mow the place down until there won't be a single rose left."

CHAPTER NINE

Monsieur Joyaux

*H*ooking François Joyaux for the two-day event at Cordovado was quite a coup on the part of Benedetta. It ensured that a large crowd of rose lovers from neighboring towns would attend. And I suspect it also raised her standing with her numerous siblings, some of whom had been skeptical about opening the family property to the public and turning the place into a rosefest.

As the guests of honor, Joyaux and his wife, Camille, were assigned the large bedroom on the *piano nobile* in the main villa at the center of the property, where Benedetta's oldest sister, Anna, lived with her husband, Sergio Gelmi. In the late nineteenth and early twentieth centuries, when Benedetta's grandfather Sigismondo Freschi ran the estate, musicians and artists of note stayed at the villa and gave performances. "In a way, we are renewing a family tradition," Benedetta told me over the phone before I drove up to Cordovado.

The other guests and speakers were distributed in smaller houses and annexes on the compound. As the appointed chaperon, I was expected to be on hand to greet the Joyaux upon their arrival, after their long car journey from the Loire Valley. But I ran into heavy weekend traffic on the way out of Venice, and by the time I reached Cordovado, the guests of honor had already settled in their lavish quarters and were having a private supper with Anna and Sergio.

I dropped off my bag in my room and joined Benedetta at the village pizzeria to go over the program for the following day. The first item on the agenda was the morning drive up to Artegna. In the afternoon, Joyaux was to give his lecture on the Gallica rose. I saw he was to be followed by another Frenchman, a certain Monsieur Frédéric d'Agay.

"What will *he* be speaking about?" I asked Benedetta.

"Antoine de Saint-Exupéry, the author of *The Little Prince*. They were related. He's a grandnephew, I believe."

"I didn't know Saint-Exupéry cultivated roses."

"He didn't."

"And so . . . ?"

"You'll see," she said mysteriously.

The high point of the two-day event—at least from my perspective—was scheduled for the morning of the second day, when Benedetta and I would take Joyaux and his wife for a walk in the woods of Alvisopoli and show them the Rosa Moceniga abloom in its natural surroundings.

We left the pizzeria and walked back to the villa through emptied streets. "I hope the roses will put on a good show," I said, bidding Benedetta good night.

Later, as I waited to fall asleep in my bed, my thoughts drifted to the mysterious Monsieur d'Agay, and in my dreamy state I wondered if he had not come to Cordovado to reveal something about the petulant rose in *The Little Prince*.

I got up early the next day and went for a walk in the garden. It was crisp and neat like an elegantly laid table. The main lawn in front of the house had been freshly mowed and now glistened with early morning dew. Potted lemon trees lined the perimeter. On the side nearer the villa, a long pergola was covered with late-blooming wisteria. All around the green rectangle,

shrubs and ramblers covered with white, pink, and red roses burst from the ground like fanciful waterworks.

Beyond the formal garden was the park that Sigismondo, Benedetta's grandfather, had designed and created in the late 1800s: a small romantic park with pretty views and easy trails. There were century-old plane trees, ilex groves, and rows of shimmering poplars; canals and bridges; narrow pathways with the occasional broken statue; and hillocks covered with spiraling boxwood hedges that led to shady belvederes.

Benedetta and her siblings had managed to preserve the grounds as their grandfather had left them, replanting old shrubs and hedges and trees where they withered and died but never altering the overall structure and appearance of the park. One of the few concessions Benedetta had allowed herself was a long, curving patch at the end of the great lawn where she'd planted roses in honor of Empress Josephine. I headed there with anticipation, knowing that old roses are at their most fragrant in the early morning hours.

There were a dozen varieties connected to Josephine in one way or another, which I tried to identify, peeking at the tag when I wasn't sure. The first I recognized was the lemony-white China stud 'Hume's Blush Tea-Scented China', which Josephine had obtained thanks to the good offices of the British Admiralty. Nearby was a tall shrub covered with languorous, pink-purple 'Jenny Duval'. Immediately behind it I saw a Chestnut rose (*R. roxburghii*), a thorny shell-pink Chinese sent to England via the British East India Company by William Roxburgh, the Scottish surgeon turned botanist who ran the botanical garden in Calcutta in the late eighteenth century.

A fine-looking 'Duchess of Portland', of a red so deep as immediately to betray its Chinese inheritance, stood proudly in the middle of the patch. Josephine had one at Malmaison—Du Pont gave it to her after importing it from a London nursery. It is a natural cross between a Gallica, a Damask, and a Chinese—a global hybrid, as it were, with European, Near Eastern, and East Asian traits. They say nature conspired to bring this rose to life somewhere near the ruins of Paestum, site of the ancient Greek temples on the Neapolitan coast. The story relates that a little plant was discovered there and given to the Duchess of Portland; eventually it became the progenitor of the Portland roses, one of the finest dynasties of hybrid perpetuals.

Next to the 'Duchess of Portland', I noticed another rose that Josephine had obtained from Du Pont: the luscious, delicately scented 'Belle Sultane'. A thick cluster of golden stamens looked extravagantly luxurious against the velvety purple-red petals. Also nearby were the two roses one most commonly associates with Josephine: the cherry-pink, finely scented 'Empress Josephine' and the blush-white 'Souvenir de la Malmaison', a Bourbon rose that was introduced in 1843, long after Josephine's time. A Russian archduke is said to have given it its name, although the circumstances are unclear. I like to think it was in memory of Tsar Alexander I's visit to Malmaison in 1814.

With some difficulty, I identified three more Gallicas: a rich, dark red 'Tuscany Superb', a pink 'Agathe Incarnata', and a 'Pompon de Bourgogne', with its clusters of miniature pink rosettes. It was not until I reached the end of the patch that I noticed a much smaller but very familiar-looking shrub covered with silvery pink roses. The size of the plant and the freshly turned soil suggested it had been the latest addition to the plot. I was so unsettled by the sight of a Rosa Moceniga in someone else's garden that I crouched to smell the fragrance, on the off chance it was an 'Old Blush'. But the sharp raspberry scent assailed me even before I could get down on my knees. Benito, the porter over at Alvisopoli, had been handing out cuttings more generously than I thought!

The Little Prince must have been in the back of my mind from the night before, because a scene from the book suddenly came to me: after crossing the desert, the young boy with the golden curls arrives in a garden of roses and, to his shock, realizes they are the same type as the rose he had left at home, on his little asteroid. I now remembered very vividly the look of disappointment that crossed the boy's face the moment he realized that his own beloved rose was not at all unique.

After breakfast, Monsieur and Madame Joyaux came down the grand staircase and to the front hall of the main villa. This time I made sure I was on hand to greet them and to make final arrangements for our drive up to Artegna. Monsieur Joyaux came across as a very personable man, without the slightest trace of that haughtiness French luminaries sometimes affect when they find themselves in Italy. He was of average height and square-shouldered; his white hair was neatly combed to the side and his gaze was sharpened by a pair of steel-rimmed glasses. Madame Joyaux, whom I knew to be of Vietnamese origins, had a natural elegance that made her stand out in the little crowd.

We drove up to Artegna in two cars. Alas, my status as interpreter did not entitle me to a seat in the first car, with the Joyaux. I found myself in the second car, in the company of Pia Pera, a journalist who had been assigned to cover the two-day event by *Gardenia,* a popular Italian gardening magazine. When we were introduced earlier that morning, her name had seemed familiar, but it was only when we were inside the car and well on our way to Artegna that I remembered the literary fracas Ms. Pera had caused a decade earlier in New York with a novel, *Lo's Diary,* in which she reimagined the story of Nabokov's *Lolita.* Dmitri Nabokov, the author's son, had accused Ms. Pera of "literary vampirism" and sued her for copyright infringement. The original publisher, Farrar, Straus and Giroux, decided not to come out with the book, and the lawsuit was settled. *Lo's Diary* was eventually published by a lesser-known house, but only after an unusual compromise was struck: Dmitri Nabokov was allowed to write a foreword in which he savaged the very novel the reader was about to read!

The ordeal was painful and deeply demoralizing for Ms. Pera—a twisted end to a labor of love. She told me she subsequently quit writing novels; left Milan, her hometown; and moved to the countryside, near Lucca, where she reinvented herself as a writer for gardening magazines.

We drove on in silence for a while, looking out at the Friulan wine country. "It was Nabokov," she said suddenly and rather wistfully, "who taught me to appreciate the enchantment of nature."

When we finally pulled up to the house, Eleonora, in a light blue dress, her fuchsia lips glistening in the late morning light, was fidgeting at the front gate. Valentino stood a few steps behind her, in a dark suit and tie. How long had they been waiting outside? As I made introductions, I noticed Eleonora was struggling to keep the excitement of meeting Monsieur Joyaux in check. "I haven't slept a wink," she whispered as I leaned over to kiss her cheek.

A few weeks earlier I had gone up to see her to make sure everything was coming along well. The winter had been especially harsh, and the garden had taken a beating. "We are behind schedule," she had fretted. "We needed more time to prune, but now we've gone from cold to hot all at once, and the plants are budding early. I've never seen anything like it. I want the garden to be at its best when Monsieur Joyaux comes around and I worry we won't make it on time."

Valentino had evidently put in extra hours so as not to disappoint his wife. The garden now seemed in fine shape, although the roses were not quite in full bloom.

"Only a few more days and they would have been at their peak," Eleonora said to me with regret.

"Monsieur Joyaux will understand," I replied.

We began the garden tour by the usual route, walking by the thirty original cultivars that Valentino had given to Eleonora on their thirtieth wedding anniversary.

"I should have bought her a necklace!" Valentino declared, as if on cue, after Eleonora told for the hundredth time the story of how she started her rose garden.

Monsieur Joyaux laughed. "*Non, non, non* . . . Thirty necklaces at least!" he exclaimed, getting into the spirit of things. The sun was shining, and the temperature was very pleasant; a lighthearted cordiality spread through the group. As we reached the first vegetable patch the simple, rustic beauty of the garden was beginning to exert its magic.

"*C'est fou*"—"It's crazy"—Monsieur Joyaux said, turning to his wife.

"Oh . . . She *does* have a beautiful garden."

"Truly magnificent."

"And look at the soil . . . the quality of it. It is really very good."

I picked up snippets of conversation as best I could and relayed them in Italian to Eleonora, who was leading the party a few steps ahead.

Monsieur Joyaux observed each rose very carefully. "*Oui . . . oui . . . oui,*" he repeated, as if checking that everything was there, in good shape, and in its proper place. He breathed in every time he said "*Oui,*" so that it sounded more like "*Ouihh . . . Ouihh . . . Ouihh.*"

We were circling the second vegetable plot when Madame Joyaux turned to me and remarked that there were no tags tied to the roses.

"Eleonora says everything is in her head," I said.

"I suppose her head is like any other head," Madame Joyaux said after a while. "A bathtub filled with water. Once all the water will have flown out it'll be nothing but an empty tub."

I led Madame Joyaux to the third patch, where the potato plants were in full bloom. Her husband was contemplating the flowery white blanket that was evenly spread out from side to side.

"Ah, le travail que cet homme doit faire!" he exclaimed in the general direction of Valentino—"How hard this man must work!"

We continued our walk, passing by surging shrubs and cascading garlands of scarlet red Gallicas and pale Damasks and beautiful white Albas. *"Ouihh . . . ouihh,"* Monsieur Joyaux said at every step. The group came to a stop at the end of the garden and found itself face-to-face with 'Dis-Moi Qui Je Suis' ("Tell Me Who I Am"), the rose that stood at the entrance of Eleonora's "orphanage."

"Ah! Un orphelinat!" Monsieur Joyaux exclaimed, moving on before I had a chance to explain. *"Ouihh . . . ouihh . . ."*

As garden tours go, this one took place at a rather brisk pace—it was over in three quarters of an hour. We were now in a hurry to get back to Cordovado in time for lunch, but when we came to a clearing, we found that Eleonora and Valentino had laid out a few plates of prosciutto and mortadella, some local cheeses, biscuits and cakes, and bottles of red and white wine and Prosecco.

Joyaux settled into a garden chair. *"C'est un jardin magnifique!"* he said, raising his glass to Eleonora and Valentino.

There was no need for me to translate. Eleonora flashed her beaming fuchsia smile. Not quite knowing what to do next, she gulped down a glass of Prosecco and resumed passing the prosciutto tray around.

On the way back I rudely pushed my way into the first car. I knew Joyaux would be speaking about his famous collection of Gallicas when we got back to Cordovado and I was eager to ask him a few questions.

R. gallica is the quintessential European rose—the only rose species whose history we can trace all the way back to the beginning. There were once as many as three thousand varieties of Gallicas, but most have disappeared over time. Today there are only three hundred left, and Joyaux has them all. Gallicas flower only once—they do not have the gene of remontancy, which was brought to Europe by China roses. I wondered how he kept his collection free of "impostors." There were many other types of roses in his garden; it seemed to me that some of his precious Gallicas were bound to cross with other roses.

"What if a rose in your collection of Gallicas suddenly begins to reflower?" I asked Joyaux provocatively.

"C'est simple. Je l'arrache," he said without flinching— "Simple. I tear it out."

*L*ater, as we gathered for lunch around the large table in the Piccolominis' dining room, I pulled up a chair next to a square-shouldered Frenchman of average height sporting a neatly cropped salt-and-pepper goatee. He was Monsieur d'Agay, Saint-Exupéry's grandnephew and the unofficial historian of his family. (The writer's mother, Marie de Fonscolombe, was d'Agay's great-grandmother).

"Saint-Exupéry was born to be a gardener," d'Agay assured me. "He used to say it all the time."

It was hard to imagine Saint-Exupéry as a gardener. To me he was the pioneering aviator who wrote three great novels about flying—*Southern Mail; Night Flight;* and *Wind, Sand, and Stars*—before writing *The Little Prince.* When World War II broke out he joined the Free French Air Force; he was already forty by then. I had always pictured him as the goggle-eyed, overweight, overage war pilot photographed by *Life*'s John Phillips as he squeezed himself into his flying suit with the help of his mechanic at the airbase in Alghero, Sardinia, in the summer of 1944.

D'Agay said Saint-Exupéry's romantic dream of being a gardener was related to his love for the family country house at Saint-Maurice-de-Rémens, where he spent his happy childhood. His mother was forced to sell it in 1931, when she could no longer afford to keep it. "He was heartbroken because he had not been able to save it."

On July 31, 1944, less than a month before Paris was liberated, Saint-Exupéry flew his Lightning P-38 on a reconnaissance mission over Grenoble. On the return journey, his plane went down over the Bay of Marseilles.

"He was much too old to fly a war plane," d'Agay observed. "He knew the Germans would take him down sooner or later."

The Little Prince appeared in 1943. After the war, it became a worldwide best seller. Millions of readers became familiar with the rose with four thorns that grew on tiny asteroid B-612, home to the boy with the blond curls. The rose was coquettish and whiney—it complained about the cold, so the little prince put a glass bell jar over it. Yet it was also affectionate in its own self-centered way, and was genuinely sad to see the boy leave on his interplanetary journey.

Readers wondered whom the rose represented.

Saint-Exupéry's widow, Consuelo Suncin de Sandoval, a fiery Salvadoran he'd met in Buenos Aires in the early 1930s, when he was running the Aeroposta Argentina, had no doubts: *"La rose c'est moi!"*—"I am the rose!" She was so determined to prove her point that when she wrote her autobiography she called it *The Tale of the Rose*.

D'Agay made a face when he told me this. "Consuelo wasn't the rose at all. She was a drama queen. Their marriage had long been over, but she wanted to play the part of the war hero's widow."

So who *was* the rose?

D'Agay said those who disliked Consuelo insisted the rose was Louise de Vilmorin, literary femme fatale of the 1920s and '30s, and Saint-Exupéry's greatest love. They were engaged in 1923, but she called the wedding off because he wouldn't give up flying and she didn't want to live her life as a widow.

Still, according to d'Agay, it wasn't Louise de Vilmorin, either.

"Then who?" I pressed.

"La rose c'était sa maman," he said. "The rose was his mother."

A German theologian trained in psychoanalysis, Eugen Drewermann, was the first to suggest that Saint-Exupéry's mother, the formidable Marie de Fonscolombe, was the rose, in a book he wrote in the 1990s called *Discovering the Royal Child Within: A Spiritual Psychology of* The Little Prince.

"After reading the book it was suddenly very obvious to me that the rose was his mother," d'Agay said. "She was a strong, intelligent woman, and very cultivated. Saint-Exupéry's artistic qualities came from her side of the family—his father, whom he lost when he was four, belonged to one of those decadent, ultraconservative aristocratic families. After the sale of the big country house, Saint-Exupéry no longer had a home. He was always on the move and never owned anything from his past except a suitcase filled with old toys. But he remained very attached to his mother, always did as she said, and always came back to her. And besides, Saint-Ex liked chasing women, and it is well-known that Don Juans are only really looking for their mothers."

With that, d'Agay got up from the table and headed toward the conference hall, where a crowd of rose lovers awaited him.

The next morning a small party met by the fountain under an old mulberry before heading off to Alvisopoli: Monsieur and Madame Joyaux, Benedetta,

Pia Pera, and I. Monsieur d'Agay appeared as well, looking smart in his tweeds.

"Bonjour!" he said, still basking in the success of his talk on Saint-Exupéry's rose the previous afternoon.

"Sorry, Frédéric, this is only for Monsieur and Madame Joyaux," Benedetta said apologetically, rushing us into the car. "We are late! The mayor is waiting for us!" As we drove out of the property, I caught a last glimpse of Monsieur d'Agay in the rearview mirror, frowning under the mulberry.

We reached Alvisopoli, after a fifteen-minute drive, to find a small crowd milling about by the entrance to the park. The mayor, Paolo Anastasia, had arrived with members of his staff, photographers, reporters, and unidentified hangers-on. Everyone, it seemed, wanted to know what Monsieur Joyaux had to say about the mysterious pink rose that grew in the woods.

"We could have brought Frédéric after all," Benedetta said with remorse.

Benito, the porter, was pacing up and down, visibly put out by the commotion. "Who asked all these people to come?" he whispered as he pulled me aside. "I thought this was a private visit!" As the self-appointed caretaker of the grounds and custodian of the Rosa Moceniga, Benito felt he was not being paid sufficient respect by local authorities, who had done so little in the past to protect those very woods. But I could see he was secretly pleased by all the hoopla.

It was a sunny day, and the cool wind blowing down from the Dolomites still carried a hint of tingling mountain air. The pathway into the woods had been cleared of debris, and the park looked lovely. A golden light filtered through the canopy. Freshwater rushed through the small canals. Tits tweeted in the gnarled boxwood hedges. Wrens and goldfinches dipped and surged over the great shimmering pond as a flush of water hens paddled about.

Benito took the lead, waddling at the head of the party that was now strung out along the path. He hurried everyone up with impatience. *"Andiamo, andiamo,"* I heard him say to the mayor with a bossy tone—move along, move along. We reached a first clearing. "There they are!" Benito exclaimed, pointing to several shrubs covered with fragrant pink blooms. There were more nearby, and farther into the woods. Everywhere one looked, there were lush pink roses staring back at us like wild creatures caught off guard by a band of intruders.

Joyaux zeroed in on the shrub nearest to him. He rubbed the leaves, rolled the hips between his thumb and index finger, and leaned down to smell the raspberry scent. *"Ouihh . . . Ouihh . . ."* Madame Joyaux stood right behind him. *"Oh, la jolie rose,"* she said—"Oh, the pretty rose." The small crowd was now gathered around Joyaux, waiting for him to say something. He had never seen this rose before, he said. But he was fairly certain that it was not the result of a mutation over time of some previously known variety—the features were much too distinct. It was probably a rose that was well known at the time of Lucia's visit to Paris two hundred years earlier but that had long since disappeared in France. *"Cette rose est un monument historique!"* he said with Gallic panache at the end of his little speech as he turned to the mayor—"This rose is a historic landmark!" Signor Anastasia, suitably impressed, turned to his aides and said the same thing in Italian.

On the way back through the woods, I caught up with Joyaux. Lucia, he said, had probably purchased the rose in the nursery of Monsieur Noisette, where she had bought most of the plants she brought back from Paris.

"Then it was probably listed in his catalogs," I suggested.

"Perhaps," Joyaux replied. "But Noisette wrote down the names of his roses without adding their characteristics. How would we know which one it is?"

Even as he was discouraging me from making a trip to the Jardin des Plantes, where the Noisette catalogs are held, I was wondering how much an easyJet flight to Paris might set me back.

The next morning, before heading back to Venice, I stopped at a newspaper kiosk in Cordovado to pick up a copy of *Il Popolo,* a local newspaper. Inside was an article by Simonetta Venturin, a reporter who had covered our visit to the woods of Alvisopoli. Next to the article was a photograph. All of us were facing the camera and squinting into the sun. Only Benito was standing sideways, on the edge of the picture, like a camp counselor showing off his charges.

CHAPTER TEN

A Chinese Garden in Umbria

On the strength of Joyaux's pronouncement—*un monument historique!*—I got in touch with the International Cultivar Registration Authority to see whether I might register the rose and make its name official. The American Rose Society serves as the ICRA for roses, so I wrote to Ms. Marily Williams, cochair of the ARS Registration Committee, and told her the story as far as I knew it.

Her reply was not encouraging:

Dear Andrea,

Unfortunately your rose falls into the category we call "found" roses and we cannot permit these roses to be formally registered [because] even though you have not been successful in identifying your rose . . . it is possible that records exist which document it.

It occurred to me that the only place where I might still find such records was in Noisette's nursery catalogs, kept in the library at the Jardin des Plantes.

Despite Joyaux's skepticism, I fixed an appointment with the Department of Rare Books and Manuscripts in the library of the Musée National d'Histoire Naturelle at the Jardin des Plantes, and flew to Paris.

The Jardin des Plantes was the brainchild of Jean-Baptiste Colbert, the powerful minister of Louis XIV who transformed what was then the Royal Garden of Medicinal Plants into a great center for scientific research—French grandeur applied to natural history. Most of the galleries and greenhouses one sees there today were built later, in the nineteenth century, but the general layout of the garden hasn't changed much since Lucia obtained her degree in botanical studies there two hundred years ago.

The entrance to the library is on rue Geoffroy-Saint-Hilaire, named for the father of French zoology; Lucia took his course on quadrupeds in the summer of 1813. A kindly librarian set me up at the long reading table and brought out *Le catalogue des rosiers, dahlia, camellia, chrysanthèmes et paeonia cultivés dans les jardins et pépinières de Louis Noisette,* a tattered little book published in 1825. The catalog lists all the roses Noisette had in his nursery: more than one thousand. Of these, sixty-four are listed as Chinese hybrids. I went down the list, but I recognized only two names—the very popular 'Mutabilis' (the rosebush of choice today at roundabouts all over the world!) and the very rare 'Ternoux'. All the rest were unknown to me and were probably extinct. Joyaux had been right: it was impossible to determine whether any one of these roses was Rosa Moceniga, because Noisette did not provide descriptive details of *any* kind, just a long list of names that were as evocative as they were meaningless—at least to me. What did the exotic-sounding 'Azélie' once look like? How sweet was the scent of 'Zénobie'? What colors did fiery 'Prometheus' have? The sheer number of lost roses contained in that list was depressing: sixty-two out of sixty-four! And this figure took into account only Chinese hybrids. The overall number of lost roses runs into the thousands.

I consoled myself with the thought that some of the cultivars on Noisette's list may yet have survived in some forgotten corner of the world, to be found one day by a caring rose lover—such as Rosa Moceniga and the rest of the orphans in Eleonora's garden. Even so, I knew, from my own difficulties and from the dismal record of Eleonora herself, that the chances of anyone's ever identifying these recovered roses and reconnecting them with their past were very slim indeed. Noisette, no doubt foreseeing what lay in store, warns the reader of his catalog that "a moment of neglect is enough to make us lose a rose just as easily as we might have acquired it."

I walked out of the library and into the gardens. It was late March and the weather was unseasonably cold, but Parisians were out on their lunch break, and joggers were running along the trails. I headed down the central pathway toward the Seine, feeling a little foolish for having come all the way to Paris for the sake of a rose and not having found a single clue.

*T*he next day, on a whim, I took the Métro to Denfert-Rochereau and headed toward rue du Faubourg-Saint-Jacques, where Noisette ran his famous nursery back in the days of Napoleon and Josephine. Going through my old notes during the flight to Paris, I had noticed that Lucia had written down in her diary not only the name of the street but the number as well— 57 rue du Faubourg-Saint-Jacques. I had Googled the address. It turned out the street still existed. More surprising, most of the street numbers had not changed.

It was a chilly, overcast morning, and I hurried along from place Denfert-Rochereau down boulevard Arago to rue du Faubourg-Saint-Jacques. Number 57 was the first large door on the right-hand side of the street. Noisette, too old to carry on his work, had sold the property in 1840 to a Monsieur Laville, who had built a school on the grounds of the old nursery. Mother Javouhey, founder of the Congregation of the Sisters of Saint Joseph de Cluny, purchased the lot nine years later. It has since served as the congregation's headquarters. Where Noisette once cultivated his roses, the sisters keep a large vegetable garden.

Across the street from number 57, behind the wall and at the top of a small hill, stands the Paris Observatory. Lucia used it as a point of reference when she drove her gig from her house in Saint-Germain-des-Prés to Noisette's nursery. It was built in the time of Louis XIV and is said to be the oldest observatory in the world. Since the wary sisters refused to let me onto their property, I walked up to the top of the small sloping park that surrounds the Observatory and tried to peer into the gardens of the congregation from that vantage point. But an outsize neoclassical palace—the sort of building Parisians call a *petit hôtel*—stood between the Observatory and the property of the Sisters of Saint Joseph de Cluny, obstructing the view. It seemed entirely out of place—as if it had been catapulted there from one of the elegant streets in the sixteenth arrondissement.

In a way, that is what had occurred. For it turned out that the building, designed by Le Boursier and completed in 1777, was once on the Champs-Élysées, on the other side of the city. Napoleon purchased it when he became First Consul; a few years later, during the empire, he rented it to Count Marescalchi, ambassador to France of the newly created Kingdom of Italy and a figure I became familiar with when reading Lucia's diary. Marescalchi, a notorious bon vivant, dazzled Parisians with his lavish entertainments. Lucia was a frequent guest. Typical diary entries read, "Spent the evening at Marescalchi's," "Danced all night at Marescalchi's," and the more intimate "Sunday supper at M.'s."

After Napoleon's downfall the palace changed hands several times. In 1929, Théophile Bader, the owner of the Galleries Lafayette, purchased the property with the idea of tearing the building down to develop a commercial space. But the building was an architectural landmark and could not be destroyed, so Bader struck a deal with the city: he would take it down brick by brick and then rebuild it exactly as before, on a plot of land next to the Observatory. The deal also specified that, in its new location, the palace was to house the Société des Gens de Lettres de France, a literary society founded by Honoré de Balzac in 1838.

Delighted to find my path obstructed by a building Lucia had known so well, I walked gingerly through the main door, pretending to be one of the guests at a rather dreary lecture on copyright law that was just then being delivered in the former ballroom on the ground floor. I was a distracted listener. As the speaker droned on, I drifted to an earlier time, when the room would have been alive with music and dancing. I pictured Lucia swishing around on the arm of "M."—two Italians living it up on the Champs-Élysées even as the empire was beginning to crumble.

*B*ack in Venice, I wrote to Ms. Williams of the American Rose Society, confessing that I had failed to find any relevant records in Paris. She suggested I make one more attempt by contacting Vladimir Vremec, a rose expert in Trieste in whom she had great trust. Vremec, a Slovene, is a well-known figure among rose collectors. His greatest achievement is a splendid rose garden he created on the premises of the old insane asylum in Trieste. He told me he had seen the Rosa Moceniga in Eleonora's garden "rather fleetingly" a few years earlier and was not in a position to identify it. "However, I know the person who can help you," he added. "She has the finest collection of Chinese roses in her garden in Umbria."

So I was soon back on the road for what turned out to be the last leg of my journey.

*H*elga Brichet lives with her husband, André, near San Terenziano, in the district of Perugia, in a country house at the top of a hillock surrounded by vineyards and olive groves. It was late April when I visited, and the day was overcast and rainy—not the perfect conditions for looking at roses.

Mrs. Brichet came out to greet me. She had the pleasantly disheveled look gardeners often have in the spring after a day's work. "Come, let's go into the garden," she said straightaway. "The rain might start again soon. We can leave the preliminaries for later."

I followed her down a gentle slope behind the house until we reached a sprawling *R. gigantea* wrapped around a pear tree. Its outstretched limbs, heavy with foliage and white roses, rested on four large bamboo poles. The five petals of the roses were very wide; the hips looked like wild apples. Graham Stuart Thomas once called *R. gigantea* "the Empress of Wild Roses." It is one of the great species from which Chinese roses originate and has very noble descendants. Teas, Noisettes, Bourbons—all these claim *R. gigantea* as their parent.

Oddly, this rose arrived in Europe only in the late nineteenth century, long after some of its illustrious progeny—including two of the four stud Chinas

('Hume's Blush Tea-Scented China' and 'Parks' Yellow Tea-Scented China')—had revolutionized the once-tranquil world of old roses. Sir George Watt, Surveyor General of India, was the first to record a sighting of the *R. gigantea,* while on a field trip in Manipur in 1882. But it wasn't until six years later that Sir Henry Collett, a botanist and an officer with the East India Company, sent a specimen to the botanical garden at Kew, after coming across a stretch of wilderness in the Shan Hills in northern Burma, which was festooned with large white flowers that reminded him of magnolias.

The *R. gigantea* bloomed for the first time in Europe in 1896, in the Botanical Garden in Lisbon, under the care of Henri Cayeux, a talented French botanist. Cayeux then crossed the *R. gigantea* with hybrid teas, obtaining remarkable results. The first of these, which came to life in 1898, he named 'Étoile de Portugal'—a gorgeous salmon-pink rose that was flowering generously near the *R. gigantea* in Mrs. Brichet's garden. A few steps away was Cayeux's most famous rose, the languid 'Belle Portugaise', obtained in 1903, with its shell-pink flowers and sensual, elongated buds. Mrs. Brichet nudged me farther down the slope, toward other splendid hybrids related to *R. gigantea*. I recognized the rich orangey-yellow petals and tapering leaves of 'Amber Cloud', a modern hybrid *gigantea* obtained by the noted Indian breeder Viru Viraraghavan. And a few steps away was a 'Sénateur Amic', a scarlet-red climber obtained by Paul Nabonnand, the great French breeder of the early twentieth century. Nabonnand named the rose after a senator of his times. As a politician of the Third Republic, Sénateur Amic hardly left a trace, yet his name lives on thanks to the lively rose that was climbing into the olive tree in front of me.

I turned toward Mrs. Brichet to express my admiration. She seemed to be contemplating her collection of *R. gigantea* hybrids as if for the first time, quietly rejoicing in the mystery of such beauty. "Isn't it extraordinary," she said after a while, nodding in the direction of the Empress of Wild Roses spread out at the top of the hill, "that all this has come to us from a rose that grows wild in the hills of southwestern China?"

Mrs. Brichet, a former president of the World Federation of Rose Societies, grew up in South Africa. Her interest in roses was kindled in her grandmother's garden near Cape Town. She pursued her university studies in Germany, during which time she went to Rome on vacation. There she met her future husband, André Brichet, a young Belgian forestry expert who worked for the UN's Food and Agriculture Organization. In the

1970s they purchased Santa Maria della Portella, their property in Umbria, a fourteenth-century priory later converted into a farmhouse. Helga and André were married in the little frescoed chapel. For several years they came up from Rome only on weekends and holidays. But in 1979, after André suffered a stroke, they moved to the country permanently.

"It was only then that I started gardening in earnest," Mrs. Brichet told me, as we made our way in the tall, wet grass. She said she soon narrowed her interest to Chinese roses. "I was attracted by their lack of pretense—a discretion that allows one to discover them at one's own pace. I hate plants that throw themselves at you." Gradually she got rid of the other roses, old and modern alike.

Around the garden, flowering lilacs and Judas trees provided a backdrop of light blue and purple-pink. We crossed an area filled with little shrubs that had yet to bloom. "This year everything is late because of the cold and the rain," Mrs. Brichet said. Just as we were exiting the patch, I noticed that one of the shrubs was covered with lovely dark pink roses. "We call it Five Yuan," she said, and went on to explain that a group of rose-hunting friends had traveled to China a few years earlier and seen this rose in the garden of the Monastery of the Ten Thousand Camellias, in Yunnan. They obtained a few cuttings and left an offering of five yuan. "It is less than one dollar," she added with a hint of disapproval at the disparity of the exchange. But she was no doubt very glad to have received a shrub from one of those cuttings.

"Have you ever seen an *R. chinensis spontanea*?" she suddenly asked as she led me up a knoll covered with more shrubs. It is, with *R. gigantea*, the other great rose species of China from which many other roses descend. With anticipation rising, I confessed that I had not. Despite its importance in the history of roses, *R. chinen-*

sis spontanea was unknown in the West until Europeans were allowed inside China following the Opium Wars of the nineteenth century. An Irish botanist, Augustine Henry, first saw it in 1883, in a narrow ravine near the Ichang Gorges in western Hubei. But Henry's discovery was published only in 1902, in *The Gardeners' Chronicle*. In 1910, Ernest Henry "Chinese" Wilson, the most celebrated plant hunter in Edwardian England, sighted it himself during a botanical expedition in northern Sichuan. Then came the collapse of the Chinese Empire, followed by civil war and the Communist Revolution. The country was again sealed off to Westerners, and remained so for much of the twentieth century. Those early sightings became legendary. Some even began to question the very existence of the rose. China gradually opened up again in the 1980s, following the rise to power of Deng Xiaoping. An enterprising Japanese botanist, Mikinori Ogisu, organized an expedition to southwest Sichuan in 1983, in the hope of finding the rose that Henry and Wilson claimed to have seen.

"I believe it was Graham Stuart Thomas who dared Mikinori to find it," Mrs. Brichet said. And find it he did, as he came upon large shrubs covered with pale pink and reddish roses in Leibo, a mountainous county in southern Sichuan. The discovery created a wave of excitement among botanists and collectors all over the world. Mikinori himself came to be viewed as one of the great rose hunters of his generation. He returned to Sichuan a few years later, and this time Mrs. Brichet went with him. "We were driving in the mountains in the county of Pingwu, in northern Sichuan, when we suddenly saw petals of the *spontanea* on the ground. We rounded the bend, and there it was, in all its glory: pink roses everywhere. We rounded the next bend, and again large shrubs with arching branches, but this time the roses were a deep red. We kept driving up, and still the roses were everywhere, in a succession of tones, from deep red to red, to various tonalities of pink and buff, all the way to the summit." Mrs. Brichet paused to catch her breath. "I shall never forget it," she said. "I felt my brain struggling to take in what my eyes were seeing—it was that overwhelming." They had stopped for a picnic and had taken many photographs before getting on their way. "Turning back and looking from a distance, we could still see the different shades of pink covering the landscape."

Mrs. Brichet brought back a cutting from that expedition which eventually grew into the tall plant we were now coming to. The branches were very vigorous, and the light green foliage was dense and shiny. The buds were creamy white, but as the roses opened up, they took on different shades of pink, some of them turning to a reddish hue.

Back in the days when the first Chinas were arriving in Europe, at the end of the eighteenth and the beginning of the nineteenth century, rose breeders and collectors had no idea that the hills and valleys in China's interior teemed with wild rose species such as *R. chinensis spontanea* and *R. gigantea*. They assumed that many of the roses that came from Chinese nurseries via Calcutta, including the stud Chinas, were wild roses rather than horticultural varieties produced to adorn the gardens of wealthy Chinese. "The Europeans were quite ignorant about Chinese roses, because traders had no access to the interior," Mrs. Brichet explained.

I gathered from our conversation that the West still has much to learn about Chinese roses; each expedition to China seems to end with at least one small discovery or another. Although the stud China model developed by Charles Hurst in the early part of the twentieth century continues to hold sway, Mrs. Brichet suggested it now feels rigid and even misleading.

'Old Blush' and the many varieties that resemble it are a case in point. These silvery pink roses are a common sight in village gardens in many parts of China. The color and general appearance are similar, but the rose varieties differ from one another with respect to foliage, habit, number of petals, or fragrance. Yet many of these different garden plants were probably shipped to Europe—naturally without name tags—where they were crossed with varieties of European origin in the hope of producing more resilient, repeat-blooming plants. The result was that the offspring, in many cases, resembled one another.

Mrs. Brichet has collected quite a number of these offspring over the years—'Old Blush' and extended family, as it were. They are grouped together in the vicinity of the old matriarch, R. *chinensis spontanea*, from which they are descended. Feeling slightly disoriented among so many Rosa Moceniga look-alikes, I went from one to the next, comparing the flowers, rubbing leaves, occasionally taking a sniff, until I came to a nameless shrub that held my attention. I circled it twice, checked the leaves and prickles, and did a rough count of the petals. At the end of my inspection I leaned down to smell the fragrance. The blooms were still wet from the rain, and anyway it was late in the afternoon, a time of day when the scent of a rose has usually faded. Yet the traces of peaches and raspberries were still there, fainter than usual and more rounded—perhaps the last perfumed exhalation before dusk.

I asked Mrs. Brichet where that particular shrub had come from. She told me she had found it on her trip to

China with Mikinori Ogisu. "We had come down the mountains after the sighting of the *R. chinensis spontanea* and were driving in the countryside in a festive mood," she recalled, "when suddenly we noticed these shrubs of pink roses growing near an old farmhouse by the road. The car screeched to a halt. We all jumped out and ran about very excitedly taking pictures and asking the farmer if we could take some cuttings. He must have thought we were mad people."

The rose—Mrs. Brichet told me—was clearly an old horticultural variety. "Dr. Ogisu asked whether the rose repeated, and the farmer said yes. And indeed, the following autumn, we had proof that the old boy had told the truth," she said, nodding in the direction of the shrub that had captured my attention.

In the preface to the catalog I had read at the Jardin des Plantes, Noisette cautioned against making "too hasty a judgment" when trying to identify a rose, "for the features can be fickle and inconstant." How true! But I had observed a good many roses of this kind along the way, and I could tell that this particular shrub was, if not the very same as the one that now grew in my garden in Venice, then one so similar as to be its brother or sister.

All along, I thought I would find the answer to the mystery of the rose's identity in documents connected to Lucia or buried somewhere in Noisette's catalogs in Paris. But an invisible hand had suddenly changed the script: in Mrs. Brichet's garden, I had come across a living relative—a lovely pink shrub from northern Sichuan—that provided my Rosa Moceniga with a connection to its ancient Chinese lineage.

"I think this might be it," I said, doing my best to control my enthusiasm.

"Hmm," Mrs. Brichet answered. Now it was her turn to circle the little shrub, observing it with renewed interest. "Hmmmm."

Just then it started to rain again. "Let's go in for a cup of jasmine tea," she said. "We can dry our feet by the fire."

"Yes, and deal with the preliminaries," I said, laughing.

*M*s. Williams of the American Rose Society must have taken pity on me. When I got back to Venice, I found the following note:

Dear Andrea,

It sounds like you have done a very thorough job of research—unfortunately with no good result as far as identification. Normally we would not be able to register such a rose but I think your case is unusual . . . I will recommend that we accept your cultivar for registration.

Delighted by her message, I wrote back asking what the proper nomenclature should be. Could I call the rose by its Italian name, Rosa Moceniga?

Ms. Williams replied that Rosa Moceniga was not acceptable because, according to the International Code of Nomenclature for Cultivated Plants, the name of a rose cultivar cannot include the name of the genus (that is, *Rosa*).

"If you want to call it simply Moceniga, then single quotes can be used," she said.

I went out into my garden in a mood for celebration. The shrub, which now came to my shoulders, was entirely covered with roses. There must have been fifty or sixty in bloom, a silvery pink cloud floating on the lawn. Then I remembered Madame Joyaux's admonition about memory and the empty bathtub. I looked around for a flat chip of wood, pierced a hole in it, and wrote the name 'Moceniga' on the rough surface. Then I took a thread of coarse raffia and tied the tag to one of the lower branches of the shrub.

ACKNOWLEDGMENTS

This book would never have been written if Paolo De Rocco, the rose planter, had not gone poking around the abandoned park of Alvisopoli one day to find the long-lost Chinese rose that Lucia Mocenigo brought back from Paris two hundred years ago. De Rocco grew deeply attached to the park. If it has survived at all—if the trees have not been cut down for timber—it is in no small part thanks to him. I am also deeply grateful to Ivo Simonella (a.k.a. Ivo the Bear) for taming that jungle for so many years and for sharing with me his intimate knowledge of the flora and fauna of those woods. Benito Dalla Via, the self-appointed caretaker of the old park, was always happy to drop his needle and thread and put aside his embroidery to go look for roses with me. Giuditta, his wife, gave me my first cutting of the 'Moceniga'—and several others since.

One of the joys of my serendipitous chase of the 'Moceniga' has been to meet Eleonora Garlant and Valentino Fabiani and spend time in their remarkable garden in Artegna. I thank them for their infinite patience and cheerfulness—not to mention the countless meals we had at the local trattoria.

Benedetta Piccolomini was an enthusiastic supporter of this project from the very start: she fed me, housed me, and drove me around southern Friuli. She was also instrumental in bringing François and Camille Joyaux to Alvisopoli to see the 'Moceniga' firsthand—a crucial development in the story. From the start, the Joyaux shared the spirit of this adventure and were very generous to me with their time and considerable knowledge.

I thank Stefano Mancuso of the University of Florence for our conversations about plant intelligence, and for running the "identity check" on the 'Moceniga' in his lab at the university. Giusi Iuston kindly drove me around her hometown of Casarsa della Delizia, where Pier Paolo Pasolini grew up and where he is buried with his mother, Susanna.

Toward the end of my quest, I had the very good fortune of meeting Helga Brichet, an experienced and generous gardener. My visit to her extraordinary collection of Chinese roses was in many ways illuminating, and I am grateful to her for patiently taking me around her lovely garden despite the wet weather. Mrs. Brichet also read the manuscript and corrected mistakes that would have had rose experts howling at me.

Most of all, I thank Deborah Garrison, my editor, for insisting that this was a little story worth writing about.

SELECT BIBLIOGRAPHY

Austin, David. *The Heritage of the Rose*. London: The Antique Collectors' Club, 1988.

Baluška, Frantšek, Stefano Mancuso, and Dieter Volkmann, eds. *Communication in Plants: Neuronal Aspects of Plant Life*. Berlin: Springer, 2006.

Beales, Peter. *Classic Roses*. New York: Henry Holt and Company, 1997.

Christopher, Thomas. *In Search of Lost Roses*. Chicago: University of Chicago Press, 2002.

Desportes, Narcisse. *Rosetum Gallicum*. Paris: Madame Huzard, 1828.

Dickerson, Brent C. *The Old Rose Advisor*. Portland, OR: Timber Press, 1992.

————. *The Old Rose Adventurer*. Portland, OR: Timber Press, 1999.

di Robilant, Andrea. *Lucia: A Venetian Life in the Age of Napoleon*. New York: Knopf, 2008.

Ducrot, Vicky. *A Garden for Roses*. Rome: I Viaggi dell'Elefante, 2001.

Gravereaux, Jules. *La Malmaison: Les roses de l'impératrice Joséphine*. Paris: Editions d'Art et de Littérature, 1912.

Griffiths, Trevor. *The Book of Old Roses*. London: Michael Joseph, 1984.

————. *The Book of Classic Old Roses*. London: Mermaid Books, 1987.

Jacob, Anny, Heidi Grimm, Wernt Grimm, and Bruno Müller. *Roses anciennes et roses sauvages*. Paris: Ulmer, 1993.

Joyaux, François. *La rose de France*. Paris: Imprimerie Nationale, 1998.

————. *La rose, une passion française: Histoire de la rose en France, 1778–1914*. Paris: Éditions Complexe, 2001.

————. *Descemet: Premier rosiériste français*. Paris: Connaissances et Mémoires, 2005.

————. *Les roses de l'impératrice: La rosomanie au temps de Joséphine*. Paris: Éditions Complexe, 2005.

Mancuso, Stefano, and Alessandra Viola. *Verde brillante: Sensibilità e intelligenza del mondo vegetale*. Florence: Giunti, 2013.

Noisette, Louis. *Catalogue des rosiers, dahlia, camellia, chrysanthèmes et paeonia cultivés dans les jardins et pépinières de Louis Noisette*. Paris: Rousselon, 1825.

————. *Manuel complet du jardinier, maraîcher, pépiniériste, botaniste, fleuriste et paysagiste*. Paris: Rousselon, 1826.

Pera, Pia. "La rosa perduta." In *Gardenia* 342 (2013).

Phillips, Roger, and Martyn Rix. *Roses*. London: Pan Books, 1988.

————. *The Quest for the Rose*. London: BBC Books, 1993.

Testu, Charlotte. *Les roses anciennes*. Paris: Flammarion, 1994.

Thomas, Graham Stuart. *An English Rose Garden*. London: Michael Joseph, 1991.

————. *The Graham Stuart Thomas Rose Book*. Portland, OR: Sagapress/Timber Press, 1994.

Thory, Claude-Antonin, and Pierre-Joseph Redouté. *Les roses*. 3 vols. Paris: Firmin Didot, 1817–24.

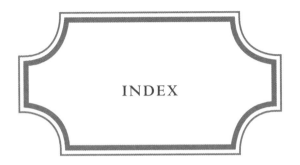

INDEX

INDEX

A NOTE ABOUT THE AUTHOR

Andrea di Robilant was born in Italy and educated at Columbia University, where he specialized in international affairs. He is the author of *A Venetian Affair*; *Lucia: A Venetian Life in the Age of Napoleon*; and *Irresistible North: From Venice to Greenland on the Trail of the Zen Brothers*. He lives in Rome.

A NOTE ABOUT THE ILLUSTRATOR

Nina Fuga is a London-based illustrator who was raised in Venice. A graduate of the Royal College of Art and a teacher of illustration at the University of Brighton and Kingston University London, Fuga works across various media, ranging from drawing to moving image. She is the recipient of multiple awards and honors in Europe, and her work is included in private collections worldwide.

A NOTE ON THE TYPE

The text of this book was set in a typeface named Perpetua, designed by the British artist Eric Gill (1882–1940) and cut by the Monotype Corporation of London in 1928–30. Perpetua is a contemporary letter of original design, without any direct historical antecedents. The shapes of the roman letters basically derive from stonecutting, a form of lettering in which Gill was eminent.

Composed by North Market Street Graphics, Lancaster, Pennsylvania
Printed and bound by Butler Tanner & Dennis, United Kingdom
Designed by Iris Weinstein